MEETING MISS IRBY

To the Reed Family,
thanks for your friendship
through the years!

MEETING MISS IRBY

JOSHUA IRBY

Denver   Los Angeles

ISBN: 978-0-9852953-1-8

Library of Congress Cataloging-in-Publication Data is available upon request.

Published by Samizdat Creative:
samizdatcreative.com

Cover design: Andrew Parker

To
my wife, Taylor,
my daughter, Israel,
my son, Elijah,
my daughter, Adeline—
the most important Irbys to me.

CONTENTS

When I came to Bosnia I met one great and good-hearted people, and the misery of these people aroused in me feelings of compassion, and I decided to give them all my life in order to heal their sufferings and to make their misery less.

—Adeline Paulina Irby (1908)

THE CAVES

Winter 1877

Into the jaws of death . . . rode the six hundred.
—Alfred, Lord Tennyson, *The Charge*
of the Light Brigade (1854)

THE HORSES, PACKED down with food, clothing and supplies, struggled to keep their footing as they ascended the steep, narrow path into the Dinaric Alps from the small Croatian town of Strmica. Their guide, an older Bosnian man, knew the path well having constructed it himself as a passage between Croatia and Hercegovina, but he could not control the forces of nature which, at the moment, were their greatest enemies. Each step forward represented progress but also made progressing more difficult, bringing higher altitudes, colder air, deeper snow, all the while the cliff dropping off abruptly just past the edge of their ribbon-thin passageway. They circumvented the remains of a violent landslide, hoping that the mountain's fury had been satisfied, and continued up an even more difficult stretch.

They were a motley troop: an old guide with a slight limp, a woman dressed in western attire, a boy, and a few men with the horses. Despite the strenuous ascent, the woman was holding her own and even seemed to be enjoying the adventure. She was the kind of traveler who finds safe and certain journeys boring; the obstructions, once overcome, impart value to the journey's end. That is not to say that she was smiling, for theirs was a mournful mission, but each of her steps seemed to rise up from the snow with the playful energy of a girl much younger.

At last, they arrived at a remote and narrow valley, through the middle of which ran a river—the waters that divided the Western world under the control of the Austrian government and the Eastern, which was now in the fiery upheaval of war. On the craggy face of the mountainside above the river was a chain of caves. Water and the natural acidity of the soil had, for ages, etched, carved, and bored their way into the limestone heart of this mountain chain, leaving the Dinara pockmarked with grottoes.

As they approached the caverns their pace slowed, allowing them time to take in the surroundings and prepare for what they would see next. The closest cave looked like the open mouth of a giant, complete with icicle teeth, and emitted a fetid smell, causing the company to come to an abrupt halt. The small fire burning about twenty feet in front of the grotto proved that they were not alone on the mountain, the very fact that had brought them from Knin to this remote place. The lady, leaving behind her paralyzed band, began walking towards the dark opening of the cave. She was middle-aged, medium build, a strong chin, square face, hair pulled back tightly and held in place with ribbons, her sensible yet clearly European dress mostly hidden beneath her winter cloak; her face, taut with determination, was not particularly attractive, but held the light of education and intelligence, and she carried herself as a noble of superior breeding and upbringing, as if she belonged on this mountain, at this moment during the depths of winter, walking into the giant's jaws. She disappeared into the darkness.

Only the old guide, still waiting beside the horses, knew what she would find in the depths of that dark cavern. Only he knew the scene that would burn itself into her memory like a brand. Only he knew that she would be unable to return unchanged to the life she had once lived. They waited. At last she emerged, the dim winter sun reflecting off of her now tear-wet cheeks and lighting the resolve in her eyes. Those tears, like the water that had carved these caverns out of the limestone wall, were percolating down into the hard places around her heart, eating away the sediment and opening up vast new reservoirs. She would need that space. Only with a large reserve of compassion and love could she endure the task that lay ahead.

This was the first and only time that anyone saw Adeline Paulina Irby cry.

MEETING MISS IRBY

*An aim in life is the only fortune worth finding—and it is not
found in foreign lands, but the heart itself.*
—Robert Louis Stevenson, *The Amateur Emigrant*[1]

FIVE DAYS BEFORE meeting Miss Irby, I found myself in a
wheelchair waiting for a ride to the hospital. It was shaping up to be a bad week. I was on the university campus
where I worked, a twenty-minute drive northwest of Atlanta,
Georgia, playing basketball with some students. Usually that
would signify a good day; I love basketball. When each player
on the team is working in concert, unselfishly giving of his
strengths and utilizing the strengths of his teammates, the
ball whipping around the court with purposeful force, the
game resembles the beauty of a symphony. Each player is a
part of the orchestra. He has trained his body to respond immediately and precisely like an instrument in a concert hall.
When the ball is shot, the trumpet blasts with muscles con-
tracting, the tympany booms with bodies fighting for position, the violin sustains as the ball hangs in the air, the snare
rolls as calves tighten for release, the cymbal crashes as the

victor snatches his prize from the air. Every rebound is a musical movement and, usually, the music is pleasing to hear.

I was guarding a player who was a mix between a wrestler and a gorilla—thick, wild, and jealous for his territory. He was winning the rebound battle, making good use of his youth and size, and I was desperately searching for his weakness. His teammate took a shot. My muscles braced for a clash and I quickly saw I had the inside position. I sent my hip violently into his gut and, with elbows out, pinned him behind me and away from the goal. My eyes followed the ball as it moved towards the rim, calculating angle and force and direction, anticipating the moment of impact. My calves drew tight, ready to recoil with enough force to send my whole body into flight, reaching the ball at its highest point. We jumped together and I knew at once I could not grab the ball with the ape on my back, so I decided to tip it away from him to where only I could get it. As gravity pulled us back towards the court, I prepared to jump again to complete the movement and take my hard-won rebound. But, as my toes touched the court and my calves contracted . . .

Pop!

I crumpled to the floor. What was to be the moving solo note of this piece came out like a French horn in the hands of a beginner—more like the dying bleat of a lamb than the clarion note of a refined instrument. I reached behind my left leg to the source of the pain. Where my Achilles tendon should have stretched—primed and taut—I found a slack cord, the useless broken string of a guitar. The concert was over.

★   ★   ★

Sitting in my house five days later, the day I met Miss Irby, the week had not gotten any better. My leg was only a small part of the problem. My life was undergoing a systematic change and the stress was difficult to bear.

In many ways, I was a typical husband and father of a typical American family. My wife and I had two young children, one boy and one girl. We lived in a typical American four-bedroom home in a typical American subdivision. In front of our house was a small yard with a flower garden on either side of the front porch. On warm afternoons, our kids played in the front yard—rolling around in the grass, riding their bikes in the driveway, kicking a ball back and forth—while we watched from rocking chairs on the porch. Often, the neighborhood children joined in. It was not unusual for eight to ten kids to be playing in our yard at one time. Most evenings we took a walk along the quiet, tree-covered streets of our neighborhood, the neighbor kids forming a human train behind us. It usually took us over an hour to complete the two-mile route; we stopped whenever we saw someone we knew.

Our house perfectly matched our lifestyle. Upstairs were three small bedrooms, two bathrooms, a living room and a kitchen. When I came home from work, I loved to sit in the living room—specifically, in the big, plump, yellow chair in the corner—and talk with my wife as she prepared dinner in the kitchen. I spent a lot of time in that yellow chair. Its position right next to a large bank of windows made it ideal for reading in the morning. It was perfectly comfortable for long conversations with friends. From the yellow chair I could also see my family, or at least pictures of them. On the living room wall we had arranged a series of family pictures—grandparents, parents, brothers and sisters—that we affectionately called "The Family Wall." The wall was bare for the first few years we lived in the house. At first, my wife and I could not agree on the best positioning for the pictures. Then we didn't have the right kind of nails. Then we were too busy. Looking at the family wall was a visual reminder that we could agree and complete a task. It also reminded me of the people I loved.

Downstairs there was a large, open room in which we could fit up to thirty people. Whenever we had large groups over, I grilled hamburgers and steak on the back porch while guest mingled throughout the house. Football games, holidays, birthdays were all reasons to invite friends over for a cookout. I even built a small fireplace on the back patio so that we could eat outside when the weather started to turn cold.

Our house was our home. It was the only home either of our children had ever known. All of that was changing.

In six months, we were leaving that home and moving to Bosnia and Herzegovina.

I was sitting in our living room with my computer on my lap looking over an endless to-do list. The checklist included impossibly large tasks such as "sell or rent house," "sell cars," "pack," and "do something with everything else." I was tempted to pick up the phone and schedule a CAT scan. Perhaps I had brain issues. Why else was I moving our family of four to a country where we didn't speak the language and our happiness was so uncertain?

I felt the arms of my yellow chair.

I love this chair.

I am going to miss this chair.

I glanced over at the family wall. The pictures had been on the wall for a month. Now they had to come down.

I am going to miss our family wall.

I am going to miss my family.

I looked down at my left leg propped up on a chair in front of me. It was wrapped in the brown temporary bandaging I had received at the Emergency Room the night of the injury. The surgery was scheduled for the end of the week. The orthopedic surgeon said he would make an incision just behind and above my ankle, fish out the two ends of my tendon and then, strand by strand, sew it back together. After ten weeks on crutches plus a year of rehab and exercise I would be back to normal.

I don't have a year! We are moving in six months! How am I going to pack up our house and prepare to move as a "uni-ped"?

I am going to miss my leg.

My computer beeped, informing me of an unread email. It was from Greg, my friend who was living in Sarajevo.

Tue, Mar 3, 2009 at 8:40 PM
I thought y'all might be interested in this. I have been reading this book called Bosnia: A Short History by Noel Malcom. Here is an excerpt:

" . . . in 1870 Miss Pauline Irby opened a girls' school in Sarajevo, funded by an English Christian organization and staffed by Protestant deaconesses from Germany;"

I thought that was pretty cool when I read it yesterday. I'm not sure if there is more information on her.

—Greg

After a moment's pause I read the message again. Yes, it said what I thought it did. I would not be the first Irby to travel to Sarajevo. A surprising turn of events.

Who is Miss Irby?

How did she end up in Sarajevo?

What happened to her girls' school?

Why have I never heard of her before?

Are we related?

I was flooded with questions. The apprehension I was feeling about our move was replaced with anticipation. Maybe we were moving to Bosnia because we were supposed to move to Bosnia. Maybe there was a larger symphony playing of which we were only an instrument, a measure, or even a note. I felt smaller and less significant, but at the same time larger and more hopeful. If Miss Irby could figure out how to move to Bosnia, maybe we could too.

I opened Google and typed "Miss Pauline Irby Sarajevo". I didn't know much about her, but I knew she was someone I wanted to meet.

A FIRST CLASS LIFE

1831-1854

Twenty years from now you will be more disappointed by the things you didn't do than by the ones you did do. So throw off the bowlines, sail away from the safe harbor. Catch the trade winds in your sails. Explore. Dream. Discover.

—Unknown[2]

CHRISTMAS WAS FAST approaching and across London people were making preparations, bustling from shop to shop, huddling under umbrellas against the cold rain. About 120 miles northeast of the capital, almost to England's eastern coast, in a country estate on the outskirts of Norwich, one family was making preparations of a different kind.

Boyland Hall, an Elizabethan mansion built in the mid-16th century, teemed with expectation. Smoke poured from the chimneys and the servants' quarters were more frantic and hurried than usual. The children were playing quietly in their rooms, but there was an unspoken intensity throughout the house. Its source: the master suite, the place from which would soon come their new brother or sister.

The master of the house and expectant father, Rear Admiral the Honorable Frederick Paul Irby, was perhaps more nervous than at any point during his illustrious naval career. He joined the Royal Navy a few months before his twelfth birthday and was an experienced seaman by the age most boys hit puberty. Three days before turning twenty he took command of his first ship.

He was best known for the battle that ended his career on the sea. His ship, the *HMS Amelia*, was patrolling the northwest coast of Africa in suppression of the slave trade when they spotted a suspicious French frigate. He ordered pursuit. Even though his sailors were exhausted and depleted from two years of service in Africa, and even though he was outgunned and outmanned, Captain Irby would not relent until at last, in the middle of the night, the French ship turned to engage.

The air was filled with smoke lit red and orange as if on fire, flashing brilliant white in the moonlight. The two warships battled for almost four hours, 78 cannons blazing, neither captain withdrawing until both ships were crippled. When at last the French frigate fled, Captain Irby was incapable of giving chase. Forty-six crewmen lay dead on the deck, 51 sat clutching their wounds, and the Amelia's rigging stood splintered like a tree after a hurricane. He returned to England seriously injured but was rewarded for his courageous leadership with recognition and, eventually, the title of Rear Admiral.

Captain Irby was from a noble, upper-class family who had been landowners in England for hundreds of years. His ancestors were knights and Parliamentarians, Barons and government officials, and it was his time to follow their example. He decided to settle down. He married Frances Wright, the beautiful daughter of a wealthy banker, and Boyland Hall, a wedding gift from her father, became their home.

However, on this 19th of December in 1831, he did not, perhaps, look like a brave sea captain. His usually fearless, handsome face was probably drawn tight with worry as he paced the smoking room. He had been married before. His wife, Emily, had died giving birth to his first child, Frederick. His son Frederick was already a grown man, but childbirth must have given rise to emotions Captain Irby never felt while giving orders from the observation deck. At sea he was in control. At sea he shouted orders and they were obeyed. But he was not at sea now, and life did not obey his orders. He could only count his steps and wait.

At last, he heard a baby's cry. The labor was over. His wife lay tired but alive on the bed, and in her arms, an early Christmas present—a little girl.

On Christmas day, in the small Protestant church on their property, their Christmas gift was baptized, Adeline Paulina Irby.

Not a lot is known about Adeline's childhood, but I expect she woke most mornings with a gleam of adventure in her freshly opened eyes. I imagine her scurrying down the stairs and across the great room, impatiently tying her bonnet as she yanked on the heavy entry door. Just outside of the arched entryway, she would cut across the front lawn and into the 150-acre wooded park adjacent to her home. There, in the refuge of the forest, she would wander, staring up at the enormous oaks and running her hand against the prickly firs. The cherry trees, however, were her favorite. When the rains let up and the sweet scent of spring beckoned her, she would climb up in a tree and pick the ripe, red cherries from the branches and plop them in her mouth, the juice running down her cheeks. On other days, perhaps she would pretend to be an explorer in a wild and dangerous land or an adventurer fleeing fiery dragons and hiding within stone castles. For a curious little girl with an active imagination in search of adventure, there were endless possibilities.

In this way Adeline was much more like her father than her mother. She was a miniature female embodiment of his sense of adventure and courage, his fearless drive to go farther and deeper and higher, his restlessness in the face of common, everyday life. Her father's spirit was contagious and Adeline was clearly infected. He had a life perspective that asked not just, "What's wrong with the world?" but "How can the world be improved?" and "How can I be a part of fixing it?" She was shaped by his principles and his passion as he threw himself into the abolitionist movement in his home county with the same fervor he fought slavery on the sea. If she could have had the opportunity, she might have run off to join the Navy too, were that something a woman could do in her day.

In the absence of personal details about the young Adeline, there is only conjecture. Did she slip into father's study where he was at his desk by the window engrossed in paperwork? Did she try to count the books that lined the high walls, stopping when she concluded that her father must be the smartest

man in the world, or at least one of the smartest men in the
world, or at least a consultant to the smartest men in the
world? Did she lean in close to the table, her chest against
the fine dinner china, ear turned towards her father? Did she
hold her breath lest the sound of breathing cover up a word,
her upper-body straining out like a cantilever hovering over
the food that had become wholly disinteresting the moment
her father began telling stories from his childhood? Did she
linger at the top of the stairs on the way to bed, cemented
in place by the voices echoing from a gathering below (perhaps, a meeting of the Norfolk abolitionist movement)? Did
she bathe in those sounds, longing to join in, and dreaming
of the day she would be old enough to sit around the fire and
discuss plans for the improvement of the world?

Adeline's father was her hero. But he was not just her hero,
he was a hero. Objectively. Certifiably. He had forsaken aris-
tocratic comfort to risk his life for country and crew until he
was physically unable to continue. In doing so, he had made a
difference in the world.

In 1813, he returned to England with three African boys.
He had rescued them from a certain end. They would have
been chained, beaten, over-worked, branded, and owned. Yet
instead, he gave them a new beginning and a different life.
At a church in Norwich he renamed them. One of the boys
would forever carry a branding of sorts. Not one given with
the sear of hot iron, but spoken over him as a reminder of his
true identity, his new identity in England. Every time someone asked him his name, he could stand straight, shoulders
back, head up, and proclaim:

"My name is Charles Fortuatus Freeman."

For he was a free man.

If only to those three boys, Captain Irby was a hero. And that is how he was depicted in the oil painting that hung in Boyland Hall alongside generations of noble figures. He is regaled in Royal Navy blue, trimmed in gold and accented with two rows of golden buttons. His shoulders, lifted high and held firm, are adorned with the epaulettes of a captain. In the background, the sea is tossed white by a growing storm, and a sail, unfurled just behind his head, is held taut by the strong wind. But he is unmoved. He looks off into the distance, relaxed yet resolute, looking past the tempest to what will follow it—the next challenge, the next battle, the next adventure.

How many hours did Adeline stand, arms loose at her side, head tilted slightly upwards, staring at the image of her father?

Just as he anchors the painting, so he must have anchored Adeline and her home.

One April morning in 1844, Adeline's home changed. She must have known it from the moment she left her bedroom— a glance from one of the maids, an odd silence in the hall or crying from the master suite. Something was not right, something was amiss.

Their home had broken free of its anchor and begun to drift out to sea. In Adeline's thirteenth year, her father died.

Adeline never wrote about this day; she rarely wrote about herself at all. Perhaps it was too difficult for her. This event surely embedded itself inside her, burrowing down into her very core, speaking into each future experience and choice, powerful and impossible to remove.

Throughout her teenage years Adeline was at home with her mother. Frances was conventional and proud, reserved and constrained, fully aware of her superior breeding, so it is no surprise that the warm-hearted and hard-headed Adeline was not at home in her new reality. An 11-year-old girl was allowed to maintain a fantasy world of sprites and fairies, but a 16-year-old of noble English birth was to have other things on her mind.

The expectation on a young lady in that day, especially a daughter of a titled peer, was that she would find someone of equal, or better, birth and settle down to start a family. The dinner parties and gala balls and social visits were designed to bring about a proper pairing.

Although she had received so many good characteristics from her father, she did not inherit his social charm or his good looks. Unfortunately for her, social grace was one of the highest traded commodities among the elite of the Victorian era. There was a right way to do everything, and stacks of etiquette books were published to make sure that young noble ladies behaved as they should.

The Lady's Guide to Perfect Gentility, published in 1856, has chapters on:

- Agreeableness and Beauty of Person, the True Foundation of Female Loveliness
- The Art of Conversing with Fluency and Propriety
- Elegant Fancy Needle-work, Knitting, Netting, Crochet, Embroidery, Etc.

In the section on excessive talking, the author warns, "Beware of talking too much; if you do not talk to the purpose, the less you say the better; but even if you do, and if, withal, you are gifted with the best powers of conversation, it will be wise for you to guard against excessive loquacity."[3]

Adeline, who seemed to believe that she had to say everything that entered her mind, must have been like a match in a dynamite factory.

The author goes on to warn, "Avoid even the appearance of pedantry. If you are conversing with persons of very limited attainments, you will make yourself far more acceptable, as well as useful to them, by accommodating yourself to their capacities, than by compelling them to listen to what they cannot understand."[4]

I imagine Adeline at dinner parties—when she wasn't debating a guest—staring out the window, her gaze mirroring that of her father in the painting, dreaming of the adventures that must lie just outside of her reach. Ships do fine without an anchor, but only when they are out at sea, sails open to the wind, cutting the water, doing what ships are made to do.

Just seven years after the death of her father, Adeline left the Norfolk countryside, but not in the way she had dreamed. During the winter, her mother died, and as an unmarried 20-year-old lady, she moved in with her married sister in London. It was this move that would lead her towards an adventure greater than any she could have imagined.

In the summer of 1851 the world came to London. The Great Exhibition was organized by Prince Albert, the husband of Queen Victoria, as a way to solidify England's position as the leader of global industry and to spread the hope of progress through technology. The exhibition hall,

nicknamed the Crystal Palace, was a triumph of human inge-
nuity. Constructed in only nine months from idea to opening,
made from wood, glass and iron, it was large enough to comfortably fit full-sized elm trees as well as the six million visitors passing through to see the exhibits.

There were demonstrations of the latest technology—steel
making, the cotton production process, the envelope machine, and a precursor to the fax machine. Even the world's
biggest known diamond was on display. Charles Darwin,
Charlotte Bronte and George Eliot were notable guests.
Literature, art, science, technology, and human progress were
celebrated. London was, as biographer Peter Ackroyd wrote,
"the greatest city on the earth, the capital of the empire, the
center of international trade and finance, a vast world market
into which the world poured."[5]

On the other side of the park from the Great Exhibition—a
one-mile walk, across the serpentine lake and out the Victoria
Gate—Adeline was settling into her new life in the city. Living
on Hyde Park with her sister Frances, she must have been excited to have the great writers and thinkers of her era spending the summer in her "backyard." However, if she grew tired
of the crowds or the heat of the city streets, she could escape
to her wealthy brother-in-law's nineteen-bedroom country
estate, Monk's Orchard, which sat on more than 1500 acres
in Surrey, a short ride outside of London. It was a luxurious
life in which boredom would seem impossible.

Yet, Adeline remained dissatisfied. She had begun to throw
herself into education—the classics, languages, and a bit of
the sciences—and in that pursuit became interested in the education of women. Joining with some other young ladies, she
assisted in a newly opened school for women; however, she

did not find joy or purpose there. She became serious and intense, wanting to do something meaningful with her life, but unsure of what to pursue.

It wasn't that the task of educating women or improving the life of the working class in London was too hard; it was that it seemed too small. She was not endowed with the simple and single-minded focus of her peers who, like a good farmer, labored consistently and faithfully in the "little" things. She had the heart of a sailor that longed for the glory that comes amidst raging tempests and roaring cannons. I imagine her sitting next to the window that faced Hyde Park, light warming her plain face as she poured over the books forming a wall around her on the desk, searching through their pages as if groping for the exit in a dark room. She knew there was a door, a door leading out of the darkness, a door she could not find, the door through which she would discover a purpose and a reason for living.

MISS IRBY STREET

*It's a dangerous business, Frodo, going out of your door," he
used to say. "You step into the Road, and if you don't keep your
feet, there is no telling where you might be swept off to.*
—J.R.R. Tolkien, *The Lord of the Rings*[6]

F OR THE FIRST few days after meeting Miss Irby, I scoured
the web for every piece of information I could find about
her. Quickly I discovered that her name was not, in fact,
Pauline Irby, but Adeline Paulina Irby. Deeper and more thorough information, however, was difficult to find. Eventually
I came across an out-of-print biography called *Miss Irby
and Her Friends* written in the 1960s by a British librarian,
Dorothy Anderson. It took a couple days to find an affordable
copy in a small used bookstore in London and a few weeks for
the copy to travel across the sea to my home. When at last it
arrived, I read it in seventy-two hours.

The 236-page biography was well written and informative,
but it was not the writing or information that held my attention. It was Adeline's life. It was her story. In the obstacles
she faced I saw some of the same obstacles I was facing. In

many of the choices she made I saw choices I needed to make. In her 150-year-old story, I was learning about my current situation.

On the second-to-last page of the book I found a paragraph that sent me rushing down the stairs of my house, hobbling as quickly as I could on my newly repaired leg. Speaking of Sarajevo in 1966, Ms. Anderson wrote, "A new street has been cut through what was her land, and that is *Misirbina ulica*. Other streets have changed their names, some not once but twice or more, in the past fifty years, but not *Misirbina* street. That name would never be allowed to change: the memory of her and her work is kept in too great a reverence in Sarajevo." At the bottom of the stairs there was a closet containing a box of travel supplies: various maps and currencies, converters and kits. I dug through it and found a map of Sarajevo that I had kept from previous trips to Bosnia and Herzegovina. Unfolding the guide and spreading it out on the table I began scanning the streets, looking for *Misirbina ulica*. Not knowing where "her land" had been, the search was unfocused and fruitless. I wasn't even sure if the street name had survived the last round of re-labeling in the '90s. Giving up, I began to explore the city that would soon be my new home, running my finger from the fountain in the Old Town down the walking street to the Catholic Cathedral and on to where the BBI mall was under construction across from the big park. Then I saw it out of the corner of my eye, directly behind the shopping center: *Mis Irbina ulica*.

The name had survived. More than that, it had become a prominent passageway starting at the City Hall and running directly behind the National Presidency building. I had walked that street many times, maybe even a hundred times.

Until that moment, I had never known the name.

My mind raced back to the first time I visited Sarajevo in 1999; the first time I ever walked down *Mis Irbina ulica*. I had recently graduated from college and was traveling Europe for the first time. Wanting to get a firsthand perspective of the city, two friends and I walked into the College of Philosophy and asked a few groups if they spoke English. Fortunately, we had chosen the faculty with the English language department and quickly found two willing helpers. It was then that I learned the true definition of hospitality. The two men were not only willing to answer our questions but also offered to show us around.

We headed towards town, trams rattling past, and crossed over into the park across the river from Skenderija where, we were informed, some of the ice events had been held during the 1984 Winter Olympics. As we skirted the piles of snow along the road, one of the guys pointed to the back of a large early-Renaissance style building—the Presidency of Bosnia and Herzegovina—and attempted to explain their country's three-president system. I nodded as if I understood, although I didn't. A few steps past the Presidency Building, waiting for the light to change, I stood right below a road sign that read *Mis Irbina ulica*. I didn't notice it.

We continued east into the oldest part of Sarajevo— Baščaršija—where we were introduced to Bosnian coffee—a dark, caffeine-rich nectar prepared in a small hand-hammered and engraved copper pot—sipped from a small ceramic and copper cup, and served with Turkish delights. For three hours we sat and traded stories. The time was more enjoyable than a novel and more informative than a history book. The next morning I left Sarajevo.

The following summer I came back for a few days with my brother. One early evening we walked down *Mis Irbina ulica* on our way back to our hostel on the hill above the Government Building, which, unchanged since the war, stood like a broken and bare reminder. We sat on the balcony that night and discussed the history we were learning about the country and the people, how tragic and complicated and surprisingly beautiful it all was.

Each time I left Sarajevo, I returned. Each time I was in Sarajevo, I walked down *Mis Irbina ulica*. In 2003, my girl-friend Taylor visited me while I was spending the summer in Bosnia. I remembered walking hand-in-hand down *Mis Irbina* on our way to town for a date. A couple days later, on a weekend excursion to the coast, I asked her to marry me. She said "yes". In 2005, we returned to Sarajevo as a married couple. For six weeks the town was our home and countless times we walked down *Mis Irbina* talking about the challenges of married life or dreaming about our future. In 2008 we brought our two young children with us. My son took his first step in our summer apartment behind the Holiday Inn. Often, pushing our stroller into town, we would cut over to *Mis Irbina* to walk in the shade of the large oak trees.

I couldn't believe it. This street had seen every season of my life and I had seen it in every season. In the winter, the naked trees seemed to shiver overhead. In the spring, those same trees clothed themselves with life. In the summer, those broad branches gave protection from the heat. In the fall, the leaves began to loosen as busy Sarajevans prepared for the first snow. I had known this street for ten years, yet I had never known its name.

Nor had I known the person behind the name.

Collapsing onto the couch, I stared at the map in silent disbelief. In only a few months Sarajevo would be home. *Mis Irbina ulica* would be less than two miles from the apartment we planned to rent. Every day I could walk in Miss Irby's footsteps.

The final months leading up to the move were full of packing and cleaning, shopping and selling, moving out and preparing to move in. When the day of our departure arrived— the bags filled and the sad farewells completed—we took our seats on the plane. My wife and I glanced at each other with a look that said, We made it. However, the journey was only just beginning.

Even before we reached the runway for takeoff, my three-year-old daughter Izzy began asking, "Are we there yet?" and my one-year-old son Elijah started crying. I was not sure how we would survive the next twenty-four hours: three planes, two transfers, and one long layover. To make matters worse, when I was placing our bags in the overhead compartment, a book fell out and onto the head of the man seated right in front of us in 29D. It was the Bible. That was the first time I ever hit someone in the head with a holy book and I think it was a first for him too. Every half hour, the rest of the flight, the man would look back at us with disgust and sigh as if asking God why he deserved a transcontinental flight in front of two crying children and a man who throws ancient manuscripts.

Unfortunately, the flight did not improve once we got into the air. Nor did it improve for the poor man in 29D. It was impossible for me to get comfortable; the airplane seat was not designed for my almost two-meter frame. To stretch my legs, I walked the aisle. However, when I sat back down, my rear hit the back of the seat sending my knees into the kidneys of Mr. 29D. His chair rattled with the blow and I thought I heard a prayer take off to heaven, "Why God? Why me?"

By the time we reached the Zagreb airport, a sleepless night later, we were exhausted. My daughter was so tired that she fell asleep at the terminal, sprawled on top of a bag that lay on the floor, her hair glued to her face with a disgusting mix of sweat and drool. At last, we boarded the final plane. As we drew near to Sarajevo, the green mountains around the city coming into view, I was filled with a burst of energy. The scene was surreal. After years of visiting Sarajevo as a tourist, I was finally a resident.

The first few days in our new apartment passed in a jet-lagged haze, our bodies adjusting six hours to Central European Time. When at last I had a free day to explore the city alone, I knew exactly where I wanted to go. A ten minute walk to the west and I arrived at the street corner behind the BBI shopping center. There, bolted to the side of an age-worn building, was the street sign, green with bold white lettering, which read *Mis Irbina ulica*. The passers-by surely thought me strange, a statue of a man staring reverently at a dirty wall. They could not understand the sanctity of that moment. This was not any street; it was her street. This was the street where she found her destiny. This was the street where she lived more than half of her life. This was the street where a grateful nation remembered her.

Silently I read the white letters again: *Mis Irbina ulica*. Miss Irby's Street. How could I have walked this street the past ten years and not known, not realized, that this road named for a national hero bears my name too?

ACROSS THE CARPATHIANS

1855-1862

*The ordinary traveler, who never goes off the beaten route and
who on this beaten route is carried by others, without himself
doing anything or risking anything, does not need to show
much more initiative and intelligence than an express package.*
—Theodore Roosevelt[7]

SOMETIME AFTER FEBRUARY 1855 Adeline made two life-altering discoveries: the addictive thrill of travel and a traveling companion named Georgina.

In many ways, Georgina Mary Muir Mackenzie was a friend specifically designed for Adeline. Born in Scotland to Sir John Mackenzie, a baronet, lawyer, and country gentleman, she was raised in the same environment of intelligence, action, culture and principle as Boyland Hall. She understood the roles and expectations of a noble lady and yet was driven, by the example of her father, towards some kind of active labor for the good of others.

Although their homes were similar, their upbringing differed on one key point: birth order. Georgina, as the firstborn of nine children, helped teach and encourage and raise her younger brothers and sisters. Adeline was the baby girl of the family. She was accustomed to older siblings caring for her. Perhaps that is why, even though she was two years older than Georgina, Adeline often called her "Aunt."

The two ladies needed each other. Adeline—headstrong and emotional, courageous yet haphazard—needed someone responsible and stable like Georgina to keep her alive and focused. Georgina, with her weak health and cautious temperament, needed someone to push her forward towards the hard but significant work she longed to accomplish.

In 1855, Georgina and her mother began spending time in London after the death of Sir Mackenzie. No one knows how they met Adeline, but soon afterwards, they were traveling together throughout Europe—Holland, Switzerland, and Italy—the usual spots for those seeking relief from the English winters.

Common and safe travel, though, was not enough for Adeline and Georgina. They had discovered a world outside of England and, with each trip, that world called out to them with a louder voice. Soon they were traveling alone, bringing only a maid to care for their needs, pushing farther from London as if searching for something. The fall of 1858, the ladies left England for an extended tour of Germany and the Hapsburg Empire. After a year exploring the city centers of the Empire, they settled on a more audacious adventure: a trek across the wilds of Slovakia and over the Carpathian Mountains to Cracow.

A journey across the Austro-Hungarian countryside, though, was not for the inexperienced traveler. There were a number of challenges Adeline and Georgina needed to consider.

First, there was the problem of language. The empire was not homogenous. They needed a translator, but what language should that translator speak? Many of the Hungarian peasants were Slavonic and did not know how to speak Hungarian. If they hired a Hungarian guide, he would most likely not know Slavonic and be unable to communicate with most of the people they would encounter. That left them in need of multiple linguists.

That is, if they could find their way. Most towns had two, if not three, names. There was the traditional name in the people's native tongue, a Hungarian name forced upon them, and then the Germanized name found in most travel logs. Even with a guidebook it would be easy to end up where they did not want to be.

If they found their way, the accommodations were roadside inns a little more comfortable than a barn. Cramped, dirty, and full of strange odors, the establishments would barely provide the rest they needed. Their "hot bath" could arrive in a bucket, a small kitchen pot, or even a wineglass. The food, although fresh and tasty, would not provide enough nutrients for the rigors of travel; they were advised to bring their own supplies. For that, they would need another cart and driver, a driver they would struggle to keep at the reins and out of the bars.

Along with this, they would potentially encounter highway robbers, narrow mountainous passages, unending delays and inclement weather.

After May 1859, one more obstacle was added. Austria and France were at war and the Austrian forces were taking losses. The Imperial government feared that Russia would take this opportunity to sow rebellion among the Slavic people of Central Europe. If the Slavs throughout Europe united under Russia, could Austro-Hungary hold together? Suspicions abounded and the police were on heightened alert.

Despite these challenges, Adeline and Georgina left Vienna in early June 1859. They were experienced travelers, fluent in German, and decided they could make the trek without a guide or translator. Wanting to travel light and to avoid delays and breakdowns, they brought along only a supply of dried soup, tea and a green umbrella to shade themselves from the sun. They had been delighted at how little information they could find in preparation for the trip. They were searching for an adventure, not a vacation.

Full of excitement and anticipation, Adeline and Georgina set out from Bratislava in a rented hay-cart. It was not long before they were breathing deeply of the refreshing mountain air and reveling in the colors of the Carpathian chain. They described the scene from atop an ancient watchtower:

> . . . the rocky glen . . . and girding crag, and cloth-
> ing champaign, the luxuriant varied forest, now
> youthful in its green of spring, and radiant with
> the glow of evening. Beyond, the mountains rising,
> one behind the another, till the eye fairly loses itself
> in tracing their waved outlines—an endless range
> of mountains, grey, green, purple, and last in dis-
> tance blue, almost viewless blue.[8]

For that view they left the crowded capitals of Europe. They could have visited Cracow by train—a fifteen-hour ride in a luxury first-class cabin—but they would have missed the beauty and adventure of this unknown countryside. As they traveled, they took thorough notes. Georgina was most interested in the history and language of the Slavonic people they encountered, writing pages on war, migration and cultural and linguistic transformation. She was more cautious than Adeline, shouting reprimands from the cart while her travel companion descended a precipice into a river gorge or ascended a mountain crag, hand over foot on the loose rock, despite a fast approaching thunderstorm.

Adeline, on the other hand, was fascinated by the ancient castles and the ghastly tales of intrigue, love, chivalry and betrayal. She recorded tales that had been passed down through generations: a cruel royal bathing in the blood of virgins to maintain her youth; a jealous step-mother who, in competition over a lover, pushed her daughter into a raging river only to later cast herself in at the same spot because of her guilty conscience; the distraught fiancé who dug a well into the stone floor of a castle in order to free his love from enslavement. She was relentless in her pursuit of adventure. No rickety ladder, life-threatening gust of wind, warning from the locals or lack of equipment could prevent her from taking in the view from the top for herself.

They were two English ladies in the most wild and savage part of the Austro-Hungarian Empire, but Adeline and Georgina could not have been happier.

After a week of exhilarating yet exhausting travel, they reached a small thermal spa—Schmocks—nestled at the base of the mountains. There, in northern Slovakia, the

Carpathians rise to their full height, straight out of the plain, as if the range was turning its back on the wearied traveler. These were the Tatra Mountains, at once the adventurer's reward and burden. As Adeline and Georgina described it:

> That first sight of the south side of the Tatra lives in our memories as the grandest we know. Picture a chain of mountain pyramids barring across your path like a wall, their base clothed with the black pine forest, their great bald granite heads uncovered in the evening light, or covered with a veil of snow.[9]

At Schmocks they planned to relax and recover before continuing across the Carpathians to Cracow. Their recovery, however, was cut short. There, beneath the Tatras, what they had been searching for found them.

There was a banging at the door. Adeline opened her eyes to a room blackened, except for the glowing coals of the stove burning next to her bed. Blinded by the darkness, her other senses were heightened. Feeling rough sheets and a lumpy bed and smelling mountain air made stale and damp by the wooden house where they lay, she knew they were still at Schmocks.

Hearing the rhythm of Georgina's sleep, she began to wonder if she had dreamed the noise. Then, from outside the door, she heard men's voices, the clank and jangle of metal on metal, and again a jarring smack as if the door was rammed with the butt of a board.

As Adeline sat up to put on a cloak she could hear Georgina doing the same. It was probably good that the room was too dark for Adeline's face to be visible, because it was taut with anger. They didn't come to this mountain retreat to be awakened in the middle of the night by strange loud noises.

When Adeline opened the door, she was not prepared for what she found—two men dressed in the bright red and dark blue of the Hungarian police, swords at their sides and rifles in hand with bayonets fixed. The gendarmes ordered them to dress and informed them that they were under arrest.

In shock, the ladies quickly clothed themselves and packed up their belongings while the policemen watched from the hallway.

"Who do they think we are?" the ladies must have thought. "Do they think we will escape out of the window?"

After searching their room and pulling apart their furniture, the policemen led Adeline and Georgina to the waiting cart which was, ironically, better than any they had enjoyed their whole journey through the Carpathians. The men brought the ladies to a nearby town where the police chief—the Beamter—was waiting to question them.

The Beamter demanded to see their passports and papers. The ladies watched with amusement as he tried to make sense of the documents that were all in English—a language that he clearly did not understand. When the ladies pointed this out, his face grew red and he rose up to full height in an attempt at intimidation.

"If you knew what you are accused of you would not be so glib," the conversation must have gone. "It is likely that spies would have their papers in an unintelligible language!"

Before he said "spies," he paused slightly as if chewing on the word, tasting its putrid flavor, then spitting it out on pronunciation.

"Spies? What do you mean?"

"The evidence is all lining up. Did you think that during a time of war we would not monitor the mail? We know you wrote to the pastor at Saint Miklos inquiring about the 'Slavonic nation'."

They had written letters to individuals in each of the towns on their path asking for information and accommodations. They had written to that pastor because he was an authority on Slavonic antiquities. At once they understood why none of their letters had arrived.

"That traitor was a leader of the Slovaks during their last rebellion and 'Slavonic nation' was the rallying cry of their party. We know how to do our job. Did you think that would not catch our attention?"

The Beamter grew more passionate with each argument; the color of his face acting as a gage to his rage. The red darkened into burgundy.

"Do you think that simply scribbling your name in the hotel register is enough to conceal your identity? You need to be more thorough than that to fool me."

Georgina immediately knew what he was referring to. As they were leaving an inn at the beginning of their trip, the owner rushed out demanding that they sign the guest book. Because they were in a hurry, Georgina wrote their names with her riding gloves on.

"Do you think we will sit back and let these dirty, backward Slavs ruin this nation? The Slavonic tongue is like the barking of dog! I wish that I never had to hear it again! And maybe one day I won't!"

The burgundy of his anger transformed into the dark purple of a bruise.

"We will not let Russia interfere in our business! And they will get no information from you! I am sending you to my superior so that your deception can be fully uncovered!"

And with that, Adeline and Georgina were carted off, again under armed guard, to the county's court, with a signed document accusing them of *panslavistic tendencies*.

From there, the only improvement was that the Austrian officials were more courteous than the bumbling *Beamter*. They were forced to ask their guards for permission to use the restroom, which they grudgingly allowed. They were left in the street in front of the courthouse for hours until Georgina demanded they be escorted to a private room. All of their belongings were searched, including the dismantling of their green umbrella to insure that no secret notes were hidden inside. They were questioned repeatedly and told that they may be held up to two or three days. Georgina was forced to undress and submit to a body search. It was an ordeal to which few English ladies of genteel rank were ever subjected.

In the end, when the court officials realized that they were, in fact, English citizens taking in some fresh mountain air the apologies came with the same force and energy as the *Beamter's* ire. They were freed and given transport back to Schmocks so they could complete their travel.

The ladies continued across the mountains into Cracow and then, by train, returned to Vienna. When they arrived back in England, the summer of 1860, they had a story to tell. Not many English ladies had been arrested as spies. But, they also had a new mission to pursue. Writing about their arrest in *Across the Carpathians*, released anonymously in 1862, the ladies concluded:

> *The first question put to us on our examination at Leutschau was, "Do you know of what you stand accused?" and our response, "If we may believe the officials at Poprad, we stand accused of Panslavistic tendencies." Apparently it did not occur to the questioner to demand if we knew what the accusation implied; had he asked this we must have answered, "No." Naturally, however, we now became desirous to learn what Panslavism really was.*[10]

The arrest at the base of the Tatra Mountains did not frighten Adeline and Georgina away from travel. In fact, it did the opposite. It gave them a new passion—the Slavic people—and a new purpose for leaving home. A year after returning from the Carpathians they were travelling again; this time to a land even more untamed and uninviting.

THE PURPOSE OF A SNOWFLAKE

*Two roads diverged in a wood, and I —I took the one less trav-
elled by, and that has made all the difference.*
—Robert Frost, from "The Road Not Taken" (1915)

THE MOST COMMON question I heard my first month in
Sarajevo was "Why did you move here?" It was a hard
question to answer in a few minutes. I was never sure what to
say. Life in America was enjoyable; I had a close community
of friends and a fulfilling job. There was nothing in the States
that I was running away from. Even though I love the green
hills of Sarajevo, the long coffees with friends and the surprising kindness of strangers, these are not enough to explain
why I moved to Bosnia. The path that led me to Sarajevo was
more complicated than one simple choice. It stretched back
decades.

I first visited Bosnia while I was living in Split, Croatia.

At the time, the student organization I was involved with
at my university in the States had a partnership with the
same organization in Croatia.

I was attending Georgia Tech because my family lived in Atlanta, Georgia, and the tuition for students from within Georgia was much lower than for students from outside of the state.

Up until my junior year of high school, my family lived in Florida. When my Dad received a job offer in Atlanta, he called us all together for a family meeting. Because all of us were in school, he wanted our opinion on the move. So, my brothers and sisters and I voted. "Yes" to go and "No" to stay. I am sure that if any of us strongly voted "No" my parents would have been reluctant to force us. But we unanimously voted to move.

I remember what I was thinking when I voted. In two weeks school was going to begin. My English teacher had assigned a summer reading list of eight classics to be read before the first day of school. I had not even opened the first one. How was I going to read eight books in fourteen days? So, I voted "Yes." If we moved, I wouldn't have to read those books.

Not a very good reason to make a big life decision.

However, had I not voted to go, my family would not have moved to Georgia, I would not have attended the same university, I would not have been involved with the same student organization, I would not have moved to Split after graduation, I would not have visited Bosnia the fall of 1999, and, therefore, would have never moved to Sarajevo.

It is frightening how much rests on an ill-placed vote.

Either I arrived here through a combination of random events, tossed about like a rudderless boat in a turbulent sea, or there was some bigger, smarter, wiser, benevolent hand at the wheel.

★ ★ ★

The Sarajevo university students I met were the ones who most adamantly questioned my move to Bosnia and Herzegovina. The conversations varied, but they most often progressed much like the following exchange I had with a Political Science student:

"Are you visiting Sarajevo?" the student asked in response to my attempt at a Bosnian greeting.

"No," I answered, "I live here."

"You live here?" he replied with a hint of disbelief.

"Yes, we moved here from the States in September."

There was a brief lull in the conversation as the student processed the confusing information.

"You are from the States," he said almost to himself. "Why did you move here?" the last word of the sentence receiving all of the emphasis.

I said something about previous trips to Sarajevo, about the Bosnian people, about the natural beauty of the country. Then I asked him about student life on his campus. Eventually, the conversation came around to what he wanted to do after graduating with a degree.

"I don't know. Get a job, if I can find one. What I really want to do is move to America."

His answer did not surprise me. I had read a statistic in the newspaper that sixty percent of young people in Bosnia wanted to leave the country forever or at least an extended period of time. I assumed that many of those polled wanted to move to the United States or Western Europe where jobs were more plentiful and, with hard work, they could improve their lives. It seemed natural for people to pursue their dreams.

"America has everything," he continued. "It is the land of opportunity. People have money in America; they drive nice cars and live in big houses. You know, the American Dream." I did know the American Dream. I had just not realized how universal it was.

Talking with some students at the College of Law on the University of Sarajevo I began to better understand this Universal Dream.

"What is the Bosnian version of the American Dream?" I asked a student during his break between classes. He was drinking a vending machine espresso from a brown plastic cup and smoking a cigarette.

"Well, our dreams aren't as big, maybe, as they are in America," he began. "A job, a family, a normal life, that is about all we ask for. I mean, I would also love to have my own place where I can be free to do what I want... Maybe a car."

"You know, in America," I added, "you can't just have one car, you have to have two. And to really have the dream, you need to have a house and not an apartment."

"Well, there is so much more opportunity in America," he said, taking a drag from his cigarette. "I just want to have a job so I can enjoy my life. Lots of students want to leave for that reason. If they can't find a happy life in Bosnia, they are going to go somewhere else looking for it."

We talked for another ten or fifteen minutes and then he headed off to class. Two other guys sitting nearby wanted to weigh in with their opinion.

"The dream is not just about having a house," the first

student suggested, "it is about having the *biggest* house. It is not just about having a nice car, but having the *nicest* car. That is the real Bosnian Dream."

His friend agreed, "Money. That is what it's all about. How can I get the most cash for the least work?"

"If you want a good life you have two options," the first guy continued, "either work for a state firm, you know, good pay and good pension, or join organized crime. Yeah, the best way to live the Bosnian dream is to be a *kriminalac* (criminal)."

They both laughed and strolled off to class.

I could understand the reaction I was hearing from Sarajevo students because I had felt the magnetic pull of the American Dream myself. It was a part of my life from birth. The real indoctrination, though, began when I arrived on my college campus for the first week of school.

We were crammed into the auditorium, wide-eyed and confused just like all the other freshmen around the world. I was attending the premier engineering school in the southeastern United States and I was not confident that I belonged. Around me sat the top students from high schools around the country—my competition in the American Dream.

At the time, a degree from my university almost guaranteed a good job and a starting salary equal to the average employee twice my age. With that paycheck I could purchase a house, a car or two, a good entertainment system, find a good-looking spouse, some cool, witty friends and eat and drink whatever I'd like on the weekends. In many ways, that engineering degree was my key to unlock the life that people worldwide scrape and steal and sweat and fight over. The dean of students walked onto the stage and the crowd became quiet. He was dressed in a well-cut suit and bore the air of success. He approached the podium.

"Welcome. I want you to take a moment to look around the room."

Pause.

"Look at the person to your left." Pause.

"Look at the person to your right." Pause.

"Only one of you will make it through to graduation."

Silence. The sound of a thousand people trying to swallow. The battle had begun. The American dream belonged to the victor.

I whole-heartedly threw myself into the college experience, trying to balance my social life with my schoolwork, but I could never escape the ever-present burden of the battle. The grades I received in college would determine the rest of my life. Or that was at least how I felt at the time.

By the end of my freshman year I was miserable. I began to question the career path I had chosen: biomedical engineering. Math and science had always been easy for me but I did not enjoy them like history and literature. They drained me. Did I really want to spend my life in a dark room somewhere designing little parts?

Just to stay sane, I started taking philosophy classes. I know that many people can drive themselves crazy studying philosophy, but it kept me balanced. The problem is that few people in the world pay you to philosophize. As my professor loved to say, "Whatever you do, don't study philosophy. It will ruin your life! You will lose your money, your friends, and someone will run off with your wife. Philosophy ruins your life." And this was from my philosophy professor.

I could feel the American Dream slipping away.

About that time I started getting involved with a student organization on campus. Many of the members were good students, but it didn't seem like succeeding in school was the most important thing to them. They saw life as more than just a big fight in which the spoils go to the victor. They talked about purpose and meaning and making a difference in the world. This sounded better to me than praying every night for my neighbor on my right and left to fail their next exam.

During my final year in college I was having lunch with a friend, John, who worked with this same student club. I was telling him how I was going to apply to graduate school and become a philosophy professor. He was eating his lunch while I talked. When I finally stopped, he said, "We are starting a new student organization in Croatia and I think you should go help us for a year."

Spending a year in Croatia had never crossed my mind. To be honest, I did not even know where Croatia was. I had never traveled outside of North America. This was not what I imagined doing with my degree.

That moment was the culmination of a battle that had raged my entire time at university. It was a battle between opposing dreams: the universal one of health and wealth and comfort versus the uncommon one of purpose and meaning. Since so few people pursued the latter, the path was full of uncertainty and insecurity. It was like Frost's two roads diverging in a yellow wood. The one beaten down with constant travel was so appealing; all my friends were there, the way was defined, the outcome was more predictable. However, the other path, grassy and wanting of wear, beckoned to a

different part of me, a part uninterested by the allure of the
American Dream, a part that believed that life offered more
than that which money can buy, a part that imagined a trea-
sure hidden behind the road's wild tangle. I had a choice to
make. After finishing university, I took the road less traveled.

That single year in Croatia extended to two wonderful and
formative years. On returning to the States, I was eager to go
back to Croatia or Bosnia and Herzegovina, to continue the
adventure I had started. Time passed quickly, though; five
years went by like a week. I married a woman who was willing to live overseas but life became more complicated: we had
kids and a house, friends and a community. We often talked
about Bosnia and our desire to move, but something held us
back from making a decision. At last, a decade after I first left
for Croatia, we packed our things for Sarajevo.

A little over a month after arriving in Sarajevo, I attended
my first event organized by the student group I came to work
with. The lecture was on success and the speaker was a state
Congressman from Colorado who also owned his own law
firm. I arrived early to have dinner with the Congressman
and help set up the auditorium.

As the event neared and students began filtering in, I began to feel apprehensive. Here I was helping organize a seminar on success but I did not feel very successful. I was studying Bosnian language twenty to thirty hours a week and
still could not conjugate simple sentences correctly. Phrases
like, "My wife, he are very pretty," and "Tomorrow, I was to
be tiring" were daily occurrences. Even simple verbs seemed

beyond my grasp. In Bosnian the verb for "writing" and "urinating" are very similar; at least once a week I would "urinate" a letter or "pee" an email.

And it wasn't just language. I wasn't feeling successful as a father. My kids were still asking about their house in America and my daughter cried every morning on the way to pre-school. When people on the street would come up to talk to the kids, they would cower behind our legs. At night they weren't sleeping well. Izzy was waking up with night terrors, something worse than a nightmare. They weren't new—she had them occasionally in the States—but more frequent. She would cry and shake and shout uncontrollably for ten minutes while we held her, sang to her and tried to keep her from hurting herself. It is the same helpless feeling you get when holding an epileptic—your finger in their mouth, your heart in your throat, waiting for the episode to pass.

Perhaps from the lack of sleep or the stress of moving, my wife and I were not getting along as harmoniously as before. You could see it in the little things—a slightly bitter tone, a glance that pulled away too soon, a silence that lingered. I was spending hours each week filling out paperwork, standing in line, organizing our finances, paying bills. *To the bank. Stamp. To City Hall. Stamp. To the shipping company. Stamp. Back to City Hall. Stamp. Tax. Stamp. To the post office. Stamp.* By the time I got home I was ready to sit on the couch and watch a movie, not engage in deep and meaningful conversation, full of "feeling words." I was bringing home the stress from the day, inviting it in and allowing it to make itself comfortable in our apartment. The problem was it was hard to fit all three of us in bed at night.

And yet, there I was organizing a seminar on success.

I recognized a guy in the back of the room whom I had met on previous trips to Sarajevo. His name was George. He was wearing a sweater with bold, horizontal stripes that widened a bit at the midsection and charcoal dress pants. His black hair, cut short and clean, glimmered from a liberal use of gel, and the look on his face was something between a scowl and smirk. He looked like, at any moment, he might either crack a joke or crack someone's jaw. He looked exactly as I remembered.

George noticed me as I approached and his expression shifted one click towards a smirk, although I was still prepared to duck if I needed to.

"So you came back," he said in perfect American English.

"Yeah, we came a month and a half ago," I answered in hobbled pre-school Bosnian.

He continued in English, "Where is the family?"

"They are at home. Too late. Kids need sleep."

"What have you been doing since you arrived?"

I started to feel bad that I had not called him yet for coffee. But, we had been so busy trying to keep our heads above the water. Maybe it was just my guilt, but it seemed to me that his expression swung back two clicks in the scowl direction.

"I learn language. I do paper. I to help the childs and the woman." Frustrated, I bailed on the Bosnian. "Yeah, we have been really busy trying to get settled, helping the kids adjust, and learning the language."

"Well, I hope you didn't come here to find a better life, because you won't find it here." George delivered this line with the same calm confidence that one might talk about the earth's rotation around the sun or the inevitability of death.

Silence. He had verbalized the big doubt that had hidden

itself in the corner of my mind. Maybe we shouldn't have moved. What if we are miserable in Bosnia? What if we find a sadness that no amount of espresso and Bosnian food can cover? What if my children grow up to become bitter and withdrawn or miserable and angry or in some other way irreparably scarred by our decision?

In that moment, though, I remembered the family vote, the first visit to Sarajevo, the yellow chair, the email from Greg, the dogged gravity that had pulled me from choice to choice and outcome to outcome, and led me, on that day, to that hall and to that conversation. This was the second time I was glad to have met Miss Irby.

In a rare moment of clarity and wisdom I answered, "We didn't come here for a better life. We came because we feel like God wants us to be here."

The Tatra Mountains, where Adeline and Georgina were relaxing the night of their arrest, are hidden behind clouds for much of the year. When these clouds grow grey, laden with moisture and tired from restraint, they unclench their cotton fists and unleash a deluge. The water usually falls as snow, softly gliding, twisting and dancing in the wind, blessing the earth with its cold, wet individuality. These frozen molecules paint white the majestic peaks, patiently awaiting the heat of mid-summer when they will be transformed and transferred to their next task—refreshing a young shoot wearied from its labor; or forming a stream that runs the backside of the range and feeds a mountain lake; or descending deep into the rock to wait a thousand years before emerging fresh and cool to quench the parched lips of a new generation; or joining a river that rushes headlong towards a precipice, hurling itself from the cliff in a wild display of abandon and beauty that only a waterfall can provide, and then continuing on and on, down and down, until at last, finding a place of rest among friends in the sea.

So the snowflake finds its purpose—to show beauty, to give life, to wait patiently, to run wild, to fill oceans, to make lakes, to color mountains. Could it have guessed the end from the beginning? Could it have known where the combination of gravity, wind velocity, wind direction, temperature, and to-pography would take it? Or did it just say goodbye to its soft, safe, cumulonimbus home and see where the journey led?

HEADLONG INTO TURKEY-IN-EUROPE

1861-1863

By the nineteenth century, chronic poverty, strained social relations, arbitrary official cruelty and bitter resentment towards Istanbul flowed through the Ottoman Empire like poisoned blood, but no other province could match Bosnia and Hercegovina for the severity of its symptoms.
—Misha Glenny, *The Balkans*[11]

If your aim be comfort, do not go to the Slavonic parts of Turkey; and if you go there seek not comfort and flattery, but to make acquaintance with the people.
—Adeline and Georgina (1867)[12]

L OOKING AT SAMUEL Augustus Mitchell's Map of Europe from 1860, Adeline and Georgina would have found, over the area known today as the Balkans, a large pink mass labeled with large bold font: Turkey-in-Europe. This pink region extended north from Constantinople along the Black Sea until meeting Russia and the Carpathian mountains; west towards the Adriatic Sea, touching Greece and the Dalmatian coast of modern Croatia; northwest all the way to the River Sava. Turkey-in-Europe was very clearly marked and defined. But what the two resolute travelers could not have learned from Mitchell's map was the culture and historical background of the citizens of Turkey-in-Europe. With no more information than the map, one could easily assume that the area was entirely populated with 'Turks,' some eastern people who had spread onto European soil almost four hundred years before. That was what most people living in England at that time believed. All because of some color and bold lettering.

The map was also insufficient to show the current state of the empire of which Turkey-in-Europe was a part. The Ottoman Empire once covered the entire Balkan Peninsula, spilling over the Sava and flowing to the very suburbs of Vienna, engulfing much of Central Europe as it moved up the Carpathian chain, bright red on the map like fresh blood. The Empire had been an unstoppable military machine that each conquest fed and made stronger as it grew from sea (Black) to sea (Adriatic) to sea (Red) to gulf (Persian) to sea (Mediterranean) to ocean (Atlantic). Although the machine demanded a payment from those it conquered, it brought order and law and economic stability to those it ruled. For many peasants in the Balkans, who had borne the weight of defending their country from the great machine, the Ottoman conquest resulted in lower taxes and opportunities that had not been available before.

However, even the Ottomans could not defy natural law. The very thing that fed the Empire—the ever growing, conquering military—began to drain its resources. The machine was growing too large, consuming too much fuel, requiring too much administration; and the area in which it needed to perform was expanding with each conquest. Each military campaign, according to Nobel Prize winning author Ivo Andrić, "only accelerated the inexorable drift towards collapse of this doomed and exhausted empire for which there was no medicine. Because both the medicine and the disease were equally fatal for it."[13] The once quick and responsive force was pinned beneath its own weight. The Empire began to recede, like water drying on paper, and the bright red faded slowly to the pink of Mitchell's map.

As Adeline and Georgina looked at the map, safe and comfortable in their London homes, they could not have seen or understood the undercurrents and eddies of Turkey-in-Europe. So they did what they so often chose to do, they packed their bags and set off for this pink region to see for themselves the life of the Slavic people under Ottoman rule.

The summer of 1862, Adeline and Georgina were in Istanbul preparing for their trip across the interior of the Balkans. The year before, they had traveled from Prague, down through Croatia, spent Christmas in Montenegro and wintered in Greece. That path was easy and safe, especially compared to what they were planning. They were heading into the heart of Turkey-in-Europe—Sofia, Belgrade, Sarajevo, Mostar. Only a few months earlier, the citizens of Hercegovina had risen up in armed revolt against the sultan with the help of Montenegro, an uprising that required imperial troops to suppress. Despite the dangers, the ladies were determined to "see those parts of Turkey least familiar to Europeans."[14] They were willing to endure more than most Europeans would to see it.

In order to make such a journey, they needed the support of the landlords, the Ottoman government. Through the consulate in Istanbul they applied to the sultan for a *firman*, an all-encompassing visa that entitled them to the assistance of local and regional government officials. Though unsure of what awaited them, they were certain that official approval would prove valuable.

Adeline and Georgina also made other preparations. They could not set out across Turkey with an umbrella and a box of soup, like they had across the Carpathians. In Istanbul they finalized their supplies: a small tent, bathtub, camping beds, silver eating utensils, straw mats, tea, wine, brandy and medicines. The tub served multiple purposes. While traveling, it could be packed as a box, complete with a lid. When stopped, the lid could be transformed into a table. The mats would be used to cover the floors of the highway-inns. The beds would make up for the furniture the inns so often failed to provide. The luggage for the three of them—Adeline, Georgina, and their maid—required four horses for transport.

When at last they received the sultan's *firman*, the ladies must have been overwhelmed with excitement and anticipation. Georgina was only 28; Adeline was 30. They were impressionable young women rushing headlong into Turkey-in-Europe. In the furnace of the Balkans they would test their western Victorian values of progress, education, and freedom. In the furnace of the Balkans, they, themselves, would be formed.

Adeline and Georgina safely crossed Turkey that first year,

but it only served to whet their appetite for more adventure. That winter, resting and organizing their notes in Greece, they were convinced that one pass through the region would not be enough. How could they accurately understand the Balkans and its resident Slavs without more time? How could they truly understand the culture without learning more of the language? How could they understand the history without visiting more of the significant sites?

They agreed on a plan: they would visit Old Serbia, the area stretching from the plain of Kosovo to Albania. In that wild and untamed region, with its ancient churches and fortresses, they could deepen their understanding of Slavic history and culture. There were also some schools they wanted to visit. They hoped to gain a clearer perspective on the condition of education in the region.

Leaving the Greek coastal town of *Salonica* (Thessalonica) the summer of 1863, Adeline and Georgina's company was larger than it was in Istanbul. They set out on rented horses led by local horsemen (*kiradgees*), assisted by a Greek courier (*cavass*) and a translator (*dragoman*), and protected by mounted, armed Turkish guards (*zapties*). Their luggage was also heavier than before. They brought along books for distribution: a supply of Bibles in the local dialect, beginning readers for the schoolchildren, works of history they had collected. Behind their saddles were tied brightly colored rugs from the Principality of Serbia, which, they had discovered, were perfect for the many breaks and breakdowns of travel. The rug—along with a thick shade tree, a cool breeze, fresh water, and a good view—made for the perfect lunch location. Around their waists they wore knives purchased in Sarajevo, the one possession certain to go missing if left out of their site.

Taking a circuitous route through Macedonia and Bulgaria, they at last came to the plain of Kosovo. That morning, the wind tossed the boughs of the oak trees and the grazing horses wandered through the dewy pasture. The sky threatened rain. Pushing forward, the wood became sparse and the grass mingled with sandy-looking soil. At mid-day, they rested at an inn beside the Sitnica River. After enjoying a coffee with fresh cream from the cattle feeding nearby, they crossed the river and continued on the road towards Priština. A little further on, they diverged towards the hills that bordered the plain to the east and their destination for the day: the village and monastery of Gračanica.

Raised up on a small hill, the beautiful Church of Gračanica—built from heavy sandstone and limestone by the Serbian King Milutin—was a concentrated combination of arches and cupolas that undulated like the wind-tossed sea. Yet it held firm and had remained so for almost six hundred years while history passed by like tempestuous waters. Originally built during the height of Old Serbia, the church stood in the center of Ottoman controlled territory.

The church, as seen from the outside, testified to what once was, but the inside attested to what was now lost. As the poor villagers ascended the hill on the way to prayers, perhaps hope surprised them as the setting sun painted the immovable limestone walls. Perhaps God would hear their prayers and look down on them with favor. Inside the narrow and dark sanctuary, they lifted their voices to the saints, begging them to see their affliction and plead their case before God. However, as the worshippers lifted their faces towards heaven, hope dissipated. The saints—who for hundreds of years had watched over those in prayer, who were engraved on the walls of the church, who were the treasured 'archive' of the monks—could not see them. Passing soldiers had gouged out their eyes and marked their bodies with bullet holes. Only Jesus had survived the disgrace, since he was painted on the ceiling, too high to reach with a sword or bayonet. The worshippers' hope gave way to anger. The saints, to whom the people had cried for hundreds of years, now seemed to cry out to them for retribution. It would have been better if the church had been burned down. The scars only served to unite the people in animosity.

During Adeline and Georgina's visit, the church was in a worse state than usual. The prior, who was too young for the position and most likely had achieved it through bribery, was in jail. At a wedding feast, after too much brandy and too much of the talking that accompanies too much brandy, the abbot found himself in a fistfight. Although he received the first blow, he delivered the last. His opponent fell hard, striking his head against something solid and was seriously injured. The prior paid for this injury, but when the man later became ill and died, he was once more arrested. Most likely it was for the purpose of extortion, but the townspeople did not seem upset with his imprisonment. The wretched monks, facing additional bullying in the prior's absence, were doing their best to maintain the church, but were severely lacking in resources.

After showing Adeline and Georgina around the church, the monks brought them next door to see the school. The ladies walked into the small, unfurnished, cell-like schoolroom and were greeted by five miserable children with torn books under their arms. The greeting they received was surprising and disappointing. Throwing themselves down at the ladies' feet, the children contorted themselves on the dirty floor in some form of groveling that, had it not been so shocking, would have made them laugh. They compelled the teacher, one of the monks from the monastery, to get the children to their feet and allow the students to demonstrate what they had been learning. When at last the young boys formed a line—their small Slavonic readers turned to the same page—they began reading in a detached, singsong unison. The ladies were not deceived. Taking the text from one of the boys, they flipped to a different page and asked him to continue. As they had suspected, he was unable to read a word. The monk's kind face turned down with shame. The children's failure, he confessed, resulted from his own ignorance. Perhaps moved by the honesty of the monk's apology or the ten little eyes staring up at them over the old, worn books, the ladies gave to each child a new reader and, to the monk, two New Testaments in Slavonic. It was a classroom without education. How could the people ever advance themselves without learning to read? How could they hold their heads up and speak for themselves when words on a page remained mysterious? How could they learn to read without trained teachers to help them?

Adeline and Georgina were disappointed in what they found. Where were the Slavic people they had described as having "fortitude, an independent spirit, self-respect, and self-restraint?[15] Where were the people of noble character they had come to find? Here they were groveling on the floor, participating in drunken brawls, and walking with their heads hung low. For these civilized English gentlewomen to see fellow human beings debasing themselves in a manner worse than slaves was appalling. Were these not brothers of the noble Slavs they had already seen across Eastern Europe?

Leaving Gračanica, the ladies made the hour and a half ride to the town of Priština, where the mayor had prepared quarters for them. The house stood on a slope, providing the ladies a view of the clustered town below. The field on the outskirts of town was dotted with the green and white tents of an Ottoman cavalry regiment. Beyond that, far over the plain, were the shadowy outlines of distant hills.

In Priština, the leader of the Christian community (*kodgia bashi*) invited the ladies to visit their school. After what they had seen at the monastery, Adeline and Georgina had low expectations. What they found surprised them. The school was spacious, clean and properly supplied as a classroom. The bright boys who filled the room could not only read, but could also draw. The walls were decorated with artwork and texts from the Slavonic Bible. The ladies were pleased.

They noticed that the school contained a large second room that was currently unused. Adeline and Georgina, knowing that the customs of the region opposed boys and girls being taught in one room, asked the schoolmaster if he planned to use the room for a class of girls. The schoolmaster informed them that there was no female teacher available. The *kodgia bashi*, whom the ladies noted was not particularly liberal-minded in respect to female education, weighed in with his opinion.

"There are many boys in our community who are still untaught," he told them. "It would not be well for the women to know how to read and write before the men."

Adeline and Georgina showed him some leather-bound books they had with them. "These are histories and records of travel written by women."

He examined the texts inquisitively, with squinted eyes and pursed mouth, eventually asking the schoolmaster to decipher the Latin scripted title for him.

"Are you sure these are neither letters nor songs?" he asked incredulously.

"Quite sure," they responded, their answer confirmed by the teacher.

"Well, if women can write books like these, we should see what ours can do," he concluded.

As they walked back through town from the school, a monk rushed up and stopped them in the street. They listened as he made his request. He lived at the monastery in Gračanica and was away when they visited. He was glad that he found them before they left town. He wanted to know if he could have a New Testament too.

While in Priština, Adeline and Georgina decided to hire new horses before moving on to the next town. They released their current guides, who let their horses out to pasture overnight and prepared to return home. The next morning, three horses were missing. When the horses' tails were found lying in the field, the guides knew that thieves were involved. They went to the town mayor to report the robbery. The mayor moved immediately into action, arresting the first two Albanian strangers the policemen could get their hands on in the market. The two horse guides were doubtful that the men who had stolen their beasts the night before would be socializing in the bazaar the next morning. Besides that, they didn't care about culprits; they wanted their horses—their livelihood— back. The mayor, satisfied that justice was complete, made no effort to find the stolen property. The ladies debated whether to intervene for the sake of their guides, but concluded that it would be unwise. They later wrote:

> *Evidently justice was beyond the mayor's functions, and all representations on our part would be considered simply as cries for vengeance. In this part of the world, if a privileged person demands justice, somebody is sure to be punished, and that promptly—whether he be the culprit or not is a matter of comparative indifference.*[16]

Adeline and Georgina knew that the Ottoman government was attempting to stop the widespread injustice. In 1856, as part of an attempt to reorganize and modernize the empire (the *Tanzimat*), the sultan promised an equal right to education, government positions and justice for citizens of all creeds. However, declaring equality was easier than enforcing equality. Adeline and Georgina found blatant disregard for the sultan's edicts: Ottoman officials enriching themselves through extortion and bribes; local mayors yielding to the will of the upper-class for fear of expulsion; city councils using the Christian "representative" to serve the coffee and fill the smoking pipes and then asking him to leave when important discussions began.

Adeline and Georgina not only saw the injustice, they also recognized the role their homeland, England, played in sustaining it. The conservative British government held firm to a pro-Ottoman position in order to maintain the balance of power throughout Europe. The English government, fearing that the Russian Empire would take land exposed by the weakening Ottoman Empire, fought alongside the sultan's troops and supplied them with weapons and intelligence. The Christian peasants had a popular song that mocked this strange relationship between England and Turkey. The song begins with the sultan writing a letter to his "bond-sister the English Queen" telling her that he is frightened to go to war because he does not have money and supplies. The Queen replies, "Dear Bond-brother Turkish sultan, fear nothing. I will make you able to fight, nay, to gain a victory!" The sultan then goes to war, encouraged, and defeats the poor peasants who were fighting without weapons, ammunitions or money. The song concludes by asking the listener if he is not astonished that a great, free nation would so quickly strengthen the sultan against a few free mountaineers who had taken up the cause of the peasant class.

Adeline and Georgina were ashamed that their fellow Englishmen remained ignorant of those living in Turkey-in-Europe while keeping such good terms with the Ottoman government. The stolen horses were a relatively small injustice, but it reminded them of their own country's contribution to the problem.

From Priština, Adeline and Georgina crossed the plain of Kosovo to the town of Vučitrn. The day after they arrived, the Ottoman mayor paid them an early morning visit. When they came out to the covered balcony to greet him, they were surprised to find him seated on a chair rather than reclining on the cushions, as was the local custom. His dress, also, was anything but local. He wore European clothing, including an enormous pink waistcoat, and carried himself according to European manners. The ladies found him intelligent and helpful. Encouraged by his openness, Adeline and Georgina asked him if they could visit the Muslim girls' school in town.

The mayor's face immediately changed and his entourage began to look about uncomfortably. This was not the first time the ladies had made the request. Their other appeals were in writing and had been answered with a variety of excuses: "the teacher is sick," "the school is not open today," "the students are on a break." The mayor, however, having no time to develop an excuse, was forced to answer honestly. He told the ladies that such a request was to be expected from civilized and enlightened travelers. The problem was with the locals who were rude and fanatical. However, if they would come to visit his wife the following day, she would show them the school.

The next day, they arrived at the prescribed hour and were ushered into the mayor's harem. The mayor's wife—an older, over-fed Turkish woman—welcomed them in and called for coffee to be served. The younger women were dressed for the occasion; Adeline and Georgina noted the white silk gauze, the green velvet, the extraordinary gold embroidery. The English ladies, however, were uncomfortable. They had dined with princes and rode horseback across the countryside, but nothing had unsettled them more than the mayor's harem. Looking into the heavily painted faces of those girls, the ladies thought that something was missing. To Adeline and

Georgina, the faces lacked the light of intelligence, a light that had been dulled through an over-abundance of leisure and the lack of stimulating conversation. They believed that even the plainest faces could be made beautiful through education.

In Istanbul, they had heard of a movement to "emancipate" the women of Turkish society. It frightened Adeline and Georgina. They later wrote:

> Till the [Muslim] woman can receive an education calculated to arm her with self-restraint and self-respect, those would indeed assume a grave responsibility who should turn her loose on Oriental society, or suddenly divest her of her present guardians, the veil and the sacred walls of the harem. One might say more than this, and assume that until the women of the Christian communities make a more creditable use of their liberty, Muslims can hardly be expected to believe that the Eastern female possesses powers of self-guidance sufficient to justify a husband's confidence.[17]

Sitting with the Mayor's wife and the crowd of young women, the ladies were reminded of that fear and the need for education.

Some of the girls brought out bundles of handmade handkerchiefs.

"Were these made at the school?" the English ladies asked.

"No," the young women replied, "at the school the girls don't work."

"Do they only read and write at the school?"

"No, all these women have been to school, but none of

them can read or write."

"Then what do the girls learn there?" the ladies exclaimed with surprise.

"To say our prayers—Arabic prayers."

"Do any of you speak Arabic?"

"No, no."

"I speak Arabic," the Mayor's wife interrupted, with an air of superiority. Then, spreading her hands over the assembly, she added with a laugh, "But these women are all Albanians."

With that, the room grew quiet.

"When will we be able to see the school?" the ladies asked the mayor's wife.

"The school?" she responded with a confused look. "The school is closed."

With those words, the Mayor's wife awakened a sense of hardheaded determination inside of Adeline and Georgina. Tired of the unending excuses, the ladies stood and declared, "We are going to the school!"

They walked out of the harem and straight into the courtyard in front of the school. There was chaos. Women were running about, children were being pushed into the classroom, a crowd of spectators was gathering. Eventually, they were allowed to enter the school. In the small den sat a row of girls on broken benches, holding dirty and torn books written in Arabic. Together they were reciting memorized prayers. After a few minutes, Adeline and Georgina were ushered out of the room.

As they were leaving, they noticed a crowd of locals discussing something at the end of the bazaar, occasionally looking up and gesturing in their direction. They quickly mounted and headed out of town, but noticed that a group

was following them just off the road. They had succeeded in
seeing the school, but had also succeeded in angering the
townspeople. Suddenly, stones came flying from the edge of
the road: first from one side and then from the other in a vol-
ley of rocks. The ladies found themselves in the strange situation of being both attacked and protected by Muslims—their
Turkish guard and Albanian policemen discharging their
weapons at the locals. At last they made it behind the walls
where they were staying, but even then, they kept the candles
unlit so the mobs could not use them to direct their aim. That
night, Adeline and Georgina sent a message to the mayor:

> All due thanks and compliments for your good in-
> tentions; but we were much surprised to find how
> little your Muslim subjects cared either for the sul-
> tan or for you. In spite of your order, we were re-
> fused to see the school, and at this we were not so
> much angry as hurt, for we had intended only to
> show a friendly civility such as we have a habit of
> paying to the Christian schools.[18]

Safely in the home of the *kodgia bashi*, Adeline and
Georgina enjoyed the company of their host family and a local priest. The priest, who they described as intelligent and
upright in bearing, defended the mayor and his difficult
position.

"You have to understand that the mayor has half a dozen
police to go up against four to five hundred locals. What effect can he have? At least he allows us to have our own school."

The school in Vučitrn contained sixteen boys. It was small,
but clean and orderly.

"We do not have a school for girls but we hope to start one soon."

"I come from Ipek " the priest's wife added proudly, "and at Ipek there is a girl's school."

"But isn't that one of the most lawless districts of Turkey?" the ladies exclaimed.

"It is, but we also have some of the 'greatest-hearted' people in Turkey. That is where Katerina lives—a woman whose equal is not to be found in the land. It was she who founded the female school."

"My wife is her relative," the priest interjected.

"Well, we will have to go to Ipek to meet her ourselves," the ladies concluded.

They did not know the danger that conclusion would lead them into.

The next morning, the mayor appeared and apologetically begged them to visit the school once more. That morning he had read the ladies' *firman* before the town council. He was determined to improve on their last experience. When the ladies told him that they wished to travel on to Ipek, he adamantly opposed them. He told them that the governor of the district had been recently murdered while trying to raise the sultan's taxes and the whole district was in confusion. He advised them not to go to Ipek with less than one hundred men. Adeline and Georgina, however, were determined.

On their way out of town, the ladies did visit the Muslim school a second time. Their reception was a contrast to the day before. They were greeted at the door with glasses of cool water and led promptly into the schoolroom. It was filled with rows of students, saying their prayers in unison. As they exited, the mayor was waiting to ask if they were satisfied. He carried himself with an additional dignity that came from having made himself obeyed. The ladies expressed their gratitude and mounted their horses to leave.

The poor mayor was in such an unenviable position, the ladies thought as the town disappeared behind them. He was stuck between the will of the government he represented and the obstinacy of the people he oversaw.

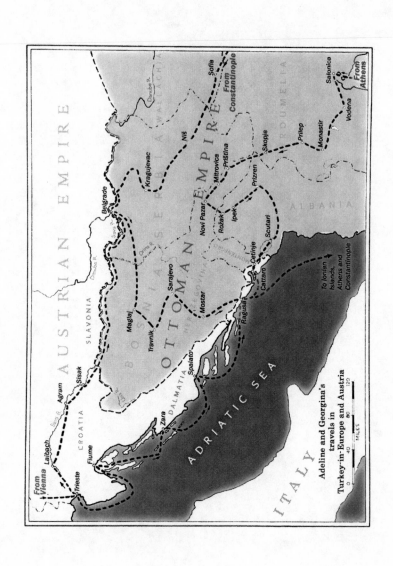

Adeline and Georgina's travels in
Turkey-in-Europe and Austria

ONE BRIGHT LIGHT

1863-1867

Such [Ottomans] as are sent to these parts are sent by their evil fate.
—Turkish Official, to Adeline and Georgina.[19]

Darkness cannot drive out darkness, only light can do that.
—Martin Luther King, Jr.[20]

IN THE BRIGHT sunshine of a July morning, Adeline and Georgina set out for Ipek (modern day Peć). Clanging and trampling alongside them was an escort of twenty men, supplied by the Governor of Novi Pazar. The white and crimson cloaks of the guards brushed against the tall grass; their weapons flashed in the sunlight and rang out through the silent hills. Into the wilds of Turkey-in-Europe they marched, not knowing that there, in the deepest darkness, they would find the brightest light.

An hour into the journey, some of the escort turned back,

having seen the ladies safely out of their district. Adeline and Georgina were relieved; perhaps the rest of their ten-hour ride would be quieter. They were quickly disappointed. From the direction of Ipek came a troop of guards sent to escort the ladies the rest of the way. The leader rode a milk-white horse and wore a scarlet tunic, bordered in gold, reaching down to his knees. The sleeves of his cloak hung so low that he had to tuck them into his waistband while riding; around his waist he wore a leather belt that held his weapons, which were inlaid with silver. On his head he wore a scarlet fez with an enormous dark-blue tassel; a silk scarf of yellow was tied around his neck. From a distance, he looked like a noble warrior, but when the ladies saw his face—sallow, sharp-nosed, cruel—they recognized his character. The ladies would later learn that he was one of the greatest villains in the whole region, stealing mercilessly from the peasants and giving his loyalty only when beneficial to him. He had been sent to escort them because he was the only one who could guarantee their safety.

Crossing the first hill they entered a mountain meadow where women were cutting hay. Little by little the path became steeper and the way more difficult, the wood giving way to rock. During one of the grimmest stretches, the guard on the white horse showed some of his true character.

"Look up at those cliffs," he shrieked in a sharp voice, waving his long, thin arm. "What power has the sultan's *firman* here, and who here has ever heard of the *Tanzimat*?"

The ladies exchanged glances, wondering whether his depreciation of the *firman* would mean anything for their safety.

"These cliffs belong to us and are inhabited by our men," he stated.

"The cliffs are quite beautiful," the ladies responded calmly. "We have seen nothing on our journey that has pleased us more." Adeline and Georgina realized that were he not assigned to protect them the sallow-faced guard would be attacking their caravan at that very moment. "It is fortunate for us, since the whole country is yours, that we have you for our guide."

The guard turned away disappointed. He had apparently wanted to impress the ladies with his importance, but they had seen through it.

At last they reached their destination, the Patriarchate of Ipek. The boastful guard, upon seeing the white walls of the monastery, clapped his spurs to his horse and road out at a gallop through the gates, his red cloak flapping in the breeze. When the ladies reached the courtyard—at that point, filled with thirty armed horsemen and foot soldiers—the monks greeted them with worried looks on their faces. The prior came forward and welcomed the ladies, but informed them that the monastery was not a suitable place for them to stay. It would be more comfortable for them if they went into town to stay with the *kodgia bashi* there.

Adeline and Georgina pulled the prior aside, away from the rabble of their entourage. "We are Christians, and do not desire to annoy you. If you wish, we will depart at once, but if you allow us to stay, we will send away all of our guards and pay for whatever we eat."

The furrows on the monk's brow cleared. "Early this morning," he told the ladies, "a troop of Albanians came through and devoured all the food they could find. They were scarcely gone when your group arrived. You are welcome to stay in the guest quarters here."

The ladies excused their guards, sending them into the town, and began settling in for the night. After a full day of travel, enduring the clanging and whooping of the troops, Adeline and Georgina were ready for some rest. However, as they prepared their room, horse hooves echoed out in the monastery and the courtyard was filled with armed men. The mayor's son had come to greet the ladies and ensure that everything was prepared to their liking. They assured him that they were satisfied. When he and his guards descended into town, Adeline and Georgina retired to their quarters.

As they slept, word spread through the region that two English women were traveling with the sultan's *firman* through Muslim country. One popular theory was that the British Queen, being a woman herself, employed women on her private errands, and had sent the ladies to evaluate the dominion of her ally, the sultan. Others believed that the ladies were queens. The rumor was out: someone important was in town.

The next morning, Adeline and Georgina received a series of visitors who had ascended the monastery hill to speak with them. The delegations included the Serbian elders of Ipek and representatives of the Roman Catholic community. It was a third group, however, that made the daily challenges of travel worth the effort.

The contingent consisted of three women, one of whom was "advanced in middle age, above middle height, with a pale calm face and singularly refined expression."[21] There was nothing outwardly noteworthy about this one woman nor was there anything particularly saintly, even though she was dressed as a nun. However, her presence altered the room. She carried herself with a humble authority and unflappable gentleness that overpowered even the most depressed environment. Her name was Katerina Simitić. She had been a wife and a mother, but both her husband and child had died, leaving her a widow and alone. She knew how to read, so, having no children of her own, she began teaching the children in her village. This work developed into a school with two classrooms: the first with twenty-seven girls who could read and write, and the second, full of young women who were studying to spend a life of "good works, teaching and prayer."[22] Adeline and Georgina were awed by Katerina and her persistence. She had succeeded in starting a girls' school in one of the wildest regions of Turkey-in-Europe. When asked how she managed to get the girls to class each day in that kind of an environment, Katerina answered, "It was difficult at first; then we decided to put up with anything rather than give up on a good purpose, trusting that God will help." When asked about the safety of the school against robbers, she responded, "Fortunately, since they already have broken in twice, the school is so poor they have little reason to rob it again." To Adeline and Georgina, she was "one of the most remarkable persons we met in Turkey, and the bravest woman we know anywhere."[23]

Katerina embodied the ladies' values and passions. She was also acting on them. These two noble Englishwomen did not come to the Balkans expecting to find someone to learn from, someone to admire, someone to emulate; this they had found in Katerina. Later, after returning to England, they would write of this encounter: "It is impossible to say how refreshing it was to converse with a woman whose mind had grasped the idea of self-devotion for the general good."[24]

Women wholly devoted to the general good were what it would take for the girls in the region to receive an education.

From Ipek, Adeline and Georgina traveled on to Prizren where they were housed in the home of the recently deceased Catholic Bishop. The ladies were glad to have such a large apartment as they found themselves constantly receiving guests from the Muslim, Catholic, and Orthodox communities. Coming from a largely homogenous Protestant country, they were profoundly influenced by their exposure to leaders and believers from all of the major faiths. They saw the divisions as a hindrance to progress in the society. Over and over again they heard the same opinion from the people:

> *However in other parts of the empire improvement may be compatible with the Turkish government, here the government is the very root of the problem. The evils that desolate the region have their source in the antagonism of races and creeds: the first aim of a good government must be to appease these rivalries; the maintenance of Turkish rule depends on fomenting them. Hated alike by Albanian and Serb, the conqueror, since the day he entered the country, has skillfully worn out the energies of his enemies by turning them against each other; should he ever allow them to make up their differences, their first act in concert would be to drive*

him from the land.[25]

They supported the rights of individuals to worship according to their customs and their language, but applauded unity whenever they saw it. When they encountered disrespect, they confronted it. While visiting a church in Prizren, they turned to see their *zaptie* wandering in through the door, disturbing those praying. They ordered him to leave with a single Turkish word. However, the guard, misunderstanding their command, grabbed two old women who had just entered the sanctuary and expelled them from the building. The other worshippers, kneeling in the dark corners or huddling around flickering candles under colorful frescoes, were not nearly as surprised by this expulsion as by the one that followed it. Adeline and Georgina walked over to the *zaptie*, removed him from the church, and with many apologies, returned the terrified women to their prayers. Extending this small justice, they had unlocked a door. A crowd encircled them, endlessly kissing their clothes, their hands and their feet, in awe that anyone, much less two women, could speak to a "Turk" that way. This honor, of course, was not what Adeline and Georgina desired, although perhaps they quietly delighted that the priest, afterwards, relaxed and spoke more openly. They had simply extended a courtesy that they felt everyone deserved.

As the ladies prepared to depart Prizren, they wanted to leave a gift with one of their hosts, a local Orthodox priest. Knowing how difficult it was to find Bibles in the local language, Adeline and Georgina gave him their last Serbian New Testament. They could not have known how welcomed the gift would be. The ladies later related the tale:

He received the book without appearance of plea-
sure, and took it home with him the evening be-
fore we left. But, the next morning he reappeared
radiant and accompanied by his wife and another
relative. He said that he had begun reading to the
women, and the language being such as they com-
monly use, the words came home to them familiar-
ly, as never in the Church-Slavonic version. They
had sat up till late, poring over the book, and now
the priest was going into the villages to read it out
to all the people.[26]

Few people understood Adeline and Georgina. They were
not queens, as the rumors told; nor were they Christians
coming to dishonor Muslim establishments, as the stone
throwing townspeople in Vučitrn concluded; nor were they
saviors planning to drive out the Turks and restore Old
Serbia, as the worshippers in Prizren might have hoped. They
were two concerned westerners, with open-hearts and open-
minds, trying to understand the complexities of a region that
few people understood.

Adeline and Georgina left Prizren and headed towards the
coast by way of the high road to Shkoder, in Albania. The
road followed the river through mountains filled with rov-
ing bands of *hajduks* (robbers) and Albanian highlanders
that even the sultan's soldiers were careful not to anger. Their
guide described these mountain men as people who "cannot be brought to order by anyone who does not belong to

themselves . . . Angry words are of no use here . . . the life of a man is of no more value than the life of a chicken."[27] When the abbot of a local monastery heard they planned to take the route over the mountains, he advised them to go another way. When the ladies ignored his warnings, the wife of the Austrian vice-Consul tried to persuade them to change their plans. A local priest had recently died on the same path when his horse slipped on the narrow road's loose rocks. Both the horse and rider fell to their deaths in the riverbed below. Added to these warnings was the story of a young Italian merchant who had caught fever during the journey and, from lack of food and proper rest, died in a dirty inn in the middle of nowhere. Adeline and Georgina had some practical reasons for ignoring this advice from friends, but most of all, as they later wrote, ". . . we had often heard of the road as traversing the wildest country in Turkey-in-Europe, and this wild country we wanted to see."[28]

So the ladies headed out of Prizren and along the Drina River on the horses of an unscrupulous guide and guarded by a group of *hajduks* they had hired to protect them from other robbers. The first few days were challenging and not without their moments of danger, but in all, nothing much more than they had already endured during previous travels. However, on the morning of the fourth day, when they were a full three days ride from Prizren and three days from Shkoder, their guide chose to show his true character. Adeline and Georgina had begun to feel the heavy-boned indication of an oncoming fever that morning. Fever was their greatest fear. They couldn't forget the stories of sickness, exhaustion and starvation they had heard. They knew that the only solution was rest.

The ladies told their interpreter to inform everyone that they would be staying in for the day in order to rest. The guide, seeing his opportunity, began yelling that if he were not immediately paid in full, he would take the horses and leave. His protests, of course, caught the attention of every bandit within shouting distance and soon there had formed a small mob of angry highlanders outside the inn where they were staying. Adeline and Georgina knew that if they paid the guide, he would leave anyway, having gotten the only thing that was keeping him loyal. Even if he didn't take off with the horse, every other *hajduk* in the region would be banging at the door with their hands out too. Once the moneybox was opened, they would be fortunate to get away with their lives. Yet, what other choice did they have? If they were left alone in the middle of this wild, mountainous country, where even the shepherds take shots at passers-by for amusement, they would not survive a night. New horses could not arrive fast enough.

Adeline and Georgina talked over their options inside of the one-room inn and decided to take a risk. They sent their interpreter out with the following message: "By demanding money now you are breaking the agreement we made before the *pasha* of Prizren, therefore we will have nothing more to do with you. Be gone! We will rest here and send for horses from the Consul in Shkoder. We will also send a telegraph to the *pasha* in Prizren letting him know how you have behaved."

The ladies anxiously listened as the *dragoman* delivered their bluff. They scarcely breathed. Then, as he delivered the last sentence, his voice grew confident, slowly enunciating the final threat. They knew that their charade had worked when they heard the guide's reply; his voice was thin and ludicrous compared to his bombastic bellowing of moments earlier. He begged their forgiveness. He had only misunderstood. Of course they would pay him in Skhoder.

The *dragoman* then added his own message, which he delivered in a condescending tone that caused the ladies to clap their hands over their mouths to stifle the uncontrollable laughter. "Well, in case those around you never before served travelers who are English, or travelers who carry a *firman*," the last word delivered slowly and with emphasis, "bid all to heart, that a *firman* entitles those who bear it to respect from every subject of the sultan; and that what English people say, they mean."

For the rest of the day, Adeline and Georgina enjoyed more peace than at any other time during their three years in the Balkans.

Adeline and Georgina eventually made it to the Adriatic coast. Afterwards, they spent Christmas in Montenegro. The following spring they made a tour of the northern Balkans visiting Austria, Slovenia, Croatia, and ending in Belgrade. The summer of 1864 they returned to England, no longer impressionable young travelers, but informed students of the region. Over a three-year period, they had crisscrossed the country five times, each journey by a different route. Back and forth over mountainous passes on horseback or riding in a springless hay cart, they had learned the Balkans, seeing modern-day Bulgaria, Serbia, Kosovo, Albania, Macedonia, Montenegro, Croatia, Bosnia and Herzegovina, Austria, Slovenia and Hungary. Little by little they had learned the language of the people, collecting and translating traditional songs, and making friends in many cities. They were influencers, ready to work to shape the perspective and policy of a nation.

Throughout their travels, the ladies were torn between their desire to help and their limited resources and influence. They did not know how to answer the endless pleas for assistance. On the day they met Katerina, one of her companions threw herself at Adeline and Georgina's feet and, through tears, told of the false imprisonment of an innocent family member. The English ladies were naturally affected by the story, but did not want to give her unfounded hope that they could help. They said to Katerina, "You must not let these poor people think that we have any influence with the Turkish authorities: they are bound to further our journey, and provide for our safety, but that is all. We are grieved to hear of your troubles, and this sad story we will mention to the first consul we meet, and relate it in our land. More we cannot do."

Katerina relayed this to the despondent woman, adding at the end, "They are friends, they will not forget us, they will tell of our troubles in their own country."[29] This addition proved truer than Katerina could have known.

In 1867, a 700 page hard-backed book including illustrations, maps and detailed appendices was published in London under the title *Travels in the Slavonic Provinces of Turkey-in-Europe* and attributed to G. Muir Mackenzie and A. P. Irby. This dense work was the result of their three years traversing the Balkan Peninsula, countless nights organizing travel notes by candlelight, and three more years of writing upon their return to England. The book was more than a travelogue; it was an impassioned and thought-out argument designed to awaken the English people to the condition of South Slavs living under Ottoman rule. Although the authors claimed in the introduction that "a political opinion of our own, of course we do not offer," it is obvious they hoped to loosen their nation's allegiance to the sultan. The book was not a complete account of their travels in Turkey; it covered only the most dangerous of their five journeys across the most lawless part of the region. This stretch of land provided the best opportunity for them to state their case: England is supporting injustice and oppression.

Adeline and Georgina were no longer tourists looking for an escape, searching for an adventure. They were diligent students, dedicated authors and outspoken advocates for the South Slav people. Still Adeline and Georgina were prepared to do more than just write a book to help their new friends.

A BIG HEART

*To love at all is to be vulnerable. Love anything, and your heart
will certainly be wrung and possibly be broken. If you want
to make sure of keeping it intact, you must give your heart
to no one . . . Wrap it carefully round with hobbies and little
luxuries; avoid all entanglements; lock it up safe in the casket
or coffin of your selfishness. But in that casket—safe, dark,
motionless, airless—it will change. It will not be broken; it will
become unbreakable, impenetrable, irredeemable.*
—C.S. Lewis[30]

AFTER SIX MONTHS in Bosnia, as the spring flowers pushed
up through the Sarajevo earth, I began to feel more at
home in my new city. Winter was over and life was gaining a
more consistent rhythm for my family. We were creating new
traditions and finding ways to enjoy old ones.

One new nightly tradition that developed, due to the lack
of children's books in English, was story time. My two children would climb into my lap and I would make up a story about whatever they wanted. At first, they took turns
choosing the topic. Eventually I became brave and started

incorporating both of their ideas into one story. Some nights it was challenging—Sleeping Beauty and Spiderman in the same tale—but I always seemed to manage.

Adeline often found her way into the bedtime stories: growing up as a "princess" in England, riding-horseback across a wild country, scaling a mountain beneath an ancient castle. Sometimes the kids even asked for it: "Tell us a story about Adeline!" Including her in the stories was a way for me to process what I was learning about her and pass on to the children some of her noble characteristics. One evening, that spring, I arrived home with the story already developed in my mind. The tale was inspired by Adeline's life and triggered by something I heard earlier that afternoon.

The comment came from a full-time student at the Law Faculty in Sarajevo. When we met, she was wearing a red, green and gold *rastacap* over her bright red hair, some of which fell across her face, resting on her glasses. During the conversation, the topic turned to Adeline and I began describing the kind of life she had in England: the town home on Hyde Park, the country estate, the servants, the high society, the comfort, the freedom. As I explained to her the benefits of upper-class life in nineteenth century London, I could tell she was impressed. Who wouldn't be? At last I told her that Adeline left it all behind to travel around the Balkans in a springless cart. She was shocked.

I asked her what she thought of someone who would leave that kind of life in London to come to Bosnia, simply because she wanted to help people. "Wow," she replied. "You have to have a big heart for that. A real big heart."

Walking home that evening the law student's words resonated in my mind: "you have to have a big heart for that."

Adeline did have a big heart, but how did it get that way? Perhaps even more importantly for me, how do I help my small heart grow?

That night when my children were ready for their bedtime story, I told them a new story:

> *There once was a loving couple waiting at home for their new baby to arrive when they heard a knock at the door. On the porch, to their surprise, were two newborns: one large, healthy baby boy and one small, sweet-faced baby girl. The boy quickly grew to be the biggest child on the playground while the girl remained tiny compared to others her age.*
>
> *The time arrived for the children to go to school so they went to the doctor for a physical exam. The physician reported back to the parents that the children were healthy, adding that he was surprised to find that both of their hearts were exactly the same size despite the obvious difference in body size. When the boy heard this, he became frightened that his heart may not be big enough for his oversized body. What if one day he wanted to love somebody and there was not enough room left in his heart? What would he do?*
>
> *He decided that he would be very picky about the people he loved. If he could find one thing about them that he did not like then he would exclude them and save that space for someone else. The*

thing was he always seemed to find some reason not to love: too tall, too short, too smart, too dumb, wrong hair color, wrong musical taste, wrong taste in food. Each time he excluded someone, his heart shrank just a little bit.

The little girl, on the other hand, knowing that her heart was big, was always looking for some reason to include others. The thing was she always seemed to find some reason to love. Each time she added someone to her heart, it grew and she found even more space for others.

One day, the boy, now a very large man, met someone in whom he could find no fault. Try as he may, he could not find a reason to exclude her. He thought to himself, "This is the one I have been waiting to love." But, when he tried to place her in his heart, she wouldn't fit. It had shrunk to the size of a green pea. With sadness, he decided that love was not for him. Not many years later, his heart disappeared with a 'poof,' and neither the very large man nor his very small heart was ever seen again.

The little girl, though, lived happily ever after.

I am not sure how big Adeline's heart was when she first arrived in the Balkans. She came to learn about the condition of the Slavic people in Turkey, but, as she saw the life of the lower class, she was motivated to help. Not because they were like her, because they weren't. Not because she agreed with them, because she didn't. Not because they deserved help, but because they needed help. And the wider she opened her heart the broader it grew.

What caused her heart to open, though? I imagine the ladies, that first year in the region, collecting facts, stories, historical events like anthropologists objectively studying a new culture, bent over their notebooks late at night recording data by candlelight. They were both well-educated students who valued knowledge. The South Slavs were a project to complete, a mystery to unravel, a question to answer. At most: an assignment. There must have been a change at some point during Adeline's three years in the Balkans; things must have become personal.

When did it change? When did the assignment become personal, the data replaced with faces? The ladies had every reason to remain objective and distant. They lived in an age when the powerful few made choices without regard to the many, the very ones bearing the weight of their decisions. Adeline and Georgina were members of that privileged class in England and enjoyed the company of nobles in every country they visited. Yet something pulled them from that high and distant vantage point. Something drew them away from the palaces of princes and into the homes of peasants. Something drew them to a people they had every reason to exclude—ethnically, financially, socially, culturally, and religiously. Something kept bringing them back again with open hearts.

The conversation with the Law student and the subsequent

bedtime story caused me to reflect on my own life. In the story, Adeline was, of course, the inspiration for the small girl with the big heart. The big man with the small heart, however, was modeled after me. I have always had a unique talent for exclusion: a discerning eye, a prejudging mind. Early on I learned to hold people to an impossible standard that even I could not live up to. It was very difficult for anyone to fit into my tiny heart. The one advantage I had as I grew older was a desire to change.

Change rarely happens overnight though. The largest shifts usually occur in secret, developing over the course of years, slowly rising to the surface from within. The gestation cycle for change seems to be at least a decade—at least, that has been my experience. You live, you struggle, you strain, you complain, you face challenges, you endure honest introspection. Then, one day, change surprises you.

Six years before meeting Miss Irby—before kids, before I was married, before deciding to move to Bosnia—I was surprised.

I was home with my family for a holiday celebration and my mom decided to clean out the basement, which was filled floor to ceiling with boxes. Some of the boxes contained treasured memories of our past—dog-eared birthday photos, bent trophies and rumpled ribbons, books once cherished and now forgotten—but most of it was worthless junk we had not taken the time to discard. This could have been done at any time, except that "my mom wanted to clean the basement" was a synonym for "my mom forced us to go clean the basement." So, on a holiday weekend, I found myself waist-deep in garbage that I had, at one point, valued so much I could not bring myself to throw it away.

Fortunately, Taylor was with me. We had known each other for less than a year but our relationship was starting to get
serious. In fact, I was keeping a secret from her. In a month
and a half I was going to ask her to marry me. The plan was
already in motion. I would be in Sarajevo with a group of college students and she was going to visit me. We would take a
weekend trip to Dubrovnik and there, next to the city walls,
I would propose. She had no idea. When she volunteered to
help me go through my share of the boxes, I assumed she just
wanted a break from the commotion of my over-sized family, but perhaps she was making sure I wasn't hiding anything
before we took the next step.

We opened the first box. To my dismay, we found a stack of
notes from old girlfriends. Taylor gave me a sideways glance
and started thumbing through the letters.

"Well, what do we have here?" she said to herself in a singsong voice.

"I wouldn't know. You're the only girl I ever think about," I
joked.

I eventually managed to extract the notes from her and
bury them deep inside the trash bag. The rest of the first box
went by without much more excitement: old cassette tapes,
schoolbooks, scraps of paper. When we opened the second
box, lying on the top of the pile was a small, faded blue folder with roughed edges. I turned the folder over. Glued to the
front was a piece of white paper shaped like an upside down
triangle or, more descriptively, a heart with only a soft inden-
tation at the top. The edges of the paper were rough, cutting
in and out like a river on a map, and on it were the names
of major cities and dots to represent their locations. It was a
country floating alone on the sea-colored folder, cut out and

removed from its neighbors. Above this island country were the handwritten words "Bosnia and Herzegovina" and below it, in the loose script of a teenage boy, was my name. I showed the folder to Taylor. She seemed as shocked as I was to find a map of Bosnia in a box that had not been opened for ten years.

"When did you make that?" she asked.

"I don't remember ever seeing this before," I responded.

Glancing down at the dot representing Sarajevo, I wondered if the Josh Irby who, years before, had created this with scissors and glue stick, could have imagined that he would one day visit?

Inside the folder were newspaper clippings glued to white, lined paper. As I read them, my memory returned in waves: freshman year of high school; history class; my teacher talking about a new war breaking out in Eastern Europe; an assignment to follow the events in the newspaper. I remembered how objectively I had searched the newspaper, cutting out articles relating to this foreign, otherworldly event. The words and the names had meant nothing to me. They were statistics and geographical locations, an assignment I needed to complete for a grade. Reading them again in my basement, they were suddenly very personal, representing events my friends had suffered through and survived. They weren't just history. They represented people, students I had met who had opened up their lives and shared their stories with me. I was more agitated than my 14-year-old self could have ever been back when I did not understand why people were fighting, why villages were being destroyed, why this white, cutout country was being torn apart. But, at that moment, in my parents' basement on Easter weekend, I was upset. And, perhaps for the first time, I realized why I continued returning to Bosnia year after year, why I wanted to do whatever I could to help, why my life's efforts always felt too small, why my grip on America and its hold on me was beginning to loosen. This was about people. This was personal.

When things get personal, life heads in strange, impulsive directions and begins demanding things that you never planned on giving. The simplest path is objectivity and exclusion. Meeting Miss Irby has not helped me stay on that path. Her story has forced me to go down into my "basement" and dig through all the junk and garbage I have collected over the years, to examine my closed, small heart and to hope for something different. Can I, like her, reject the simplest path for the better one?

SARAJEVO ROSE

1865-1872

The air of Bosnia smells like a rose.[31]

Bilo gdje da krenem (Wherever I go)
o tebi sanjam (I dream about you)
putevi me svi tebi vode, (all paths lead me to you)
čekam s nekom čeznjom (I wait with yearning)
na svijetla tvoja (for your lights)
Sarajevo ljubavi moja. (Sarajevo, my love)
—Bosnian folk song, "Sarajevo Ljubavi Moja"

SARAJEVO IS A rose growing in a valley. She rises up in the morning fog like a dreamer from her blankets, the sun transforming minarets into glowing candles and windows into flashes of fire. Her cobblestone streets, wet from their dawn washing, coax visitors to a slower pace. Her air carries the smell of fresh pastries and early morning *pita*˙. She is finely dressed, wearing history as her garments: the roughly hewn stones and dark wood of the Ottomans, the order and artistry of the Austro-Hungarians, the simplicity and function of the former Yugoslavia, and the glass-covered audacity of the post-war era. In the square mile that represents her heart, each of her major religions is represented. But, modern Sarajevo is very different from the city Adeline and Georgina encountered over a century and a half ago.

Their visit was long before the Avaz tower rose above Koševsko Brdo with its unprecedented views and the BBI Centar introduced Bosnia to the western shopping mall; long before Dobrinja, Skenderija, the Holiday Inn, and Ciglane were added in the city's rapid preparations for the 1984 Olympics; long before houses began creeping up the mountains in response to the city's growing population; long before the large block apartments were built to accommodate Yugoslavian workers, long before Marin Dvor became the outermost part of town. The ladies came to Sarajevo before stone replaced wood, pavement was laid over cobblestone, trams replaced horses, and three-story European buildings replaced small Turkish structures. The Sarajevo they discovered did not include the government and religious structures of Josip Vancaš, or the neo-Orientalist City Hall of Karl Wittek, or the multicultural vision of Kalay. The valley was not yet diversified; the citizens lived in religiously homogenous *mahalas* radiating up the hills from the city's center, from Baščaršija. Sarajevo was still firmly oriented eastward. But change was awakening. They arrived in the time

---

˙   Traditional Bosnian pie

of Topal Šerif Oman Paša, who began implementing new laws for transportation, industry, education, and government that would provide increased freedom and safety to the twenty thousand citizens of Sarajevo and open the door for two Englishwomen to open a school for girls in the city.

Following their return from Turkey-in-Europe, Adeline and Georgina were busy. While preparing their travel manuscripts, they began to discuss what they could do for their new Slav friends. As they looked back over their three-year journey, Bosnia seemed to be the area most in need of help. They estimated that in the whole country, only one percent could read, and in Sarajevo, the principle town, there was not a single bookstore. Education was particularly weak among the women of the Christian peasant class. Each village needed its own school in which girls could learn to read and write, knowledge that they could later pass on to their family as mothers. But how could they start schools without teachers? What Bosnia desperately needed was a school for training teachers. The need was clear, but how two women from England could meet that need was not.

In the summer of 1865 they took the first steps towards this goal by founding the Association for the Promotion of Education among the South Slavonic Christians in Bosnia and Herzegovina. They were joined in this association by some prominent religious leaders and members of missionary societies: the Archbishops of Canterbury and York; Lord Shaftesbury, former parliamentarian and leader of the Evangelical movement within the Anglican Church; Dr.

Norman MacLeod, the editor of the widely popular monthly magazine *Good Words*. The Association, once formed, began appealing to the public for the money required to start a school. The ladies gave liberally of their own time and money, adding to the fund all the money they received from their writings and publications and even appealing to their families for donations. Despite their efforts, progress was slow and by 1866 they had raised enough money to buy land and build a school building, but not enough to pay teachers and maintain the institution.

Adeline began visiting other organizations and associations, collecting ideas and practices in the field of education. In Germany, she found a solution to their financial problem. While spending time in the Institute of Protestant Deaconesses at Kaiserswerth, Adeline learned of their work establishing orphanages and schools throughout Turkey. She and Georgina made a proposition to the superintendent, Pastor Fliedner: they would provide the land and a school building in Sarajevo, if the Institution would supply the teachers and the funds to maintain the work. The pastor agreed and both parties went immediately to work. By the end of 1868, with the help of the English and Prussian Consuls, construction of the new school began on a piece of land that ran from Pod Musalom street to the Miljacka River, at the river bend beyond the Čumurija bridge.

Although the teachers sent by the Institution were deaconesses of a Protestant religious order, and the funds for the project came from Protestant donors in England, Adeline and Georgina were insistent that the education, offered free of charge, be made available to all who asked, whether they be Orthodox, Catholic or Muslim. It was not their intent to exclude anyone. The school was not to be a fortress with impenetrable walls, but a fire around which all who desired warmth could gather.

On August 4, 1869, in the presence of the European consulate and a collection of prominent Sarajevans, a proclamation from the Porte was read, granting permission for the establishment of the school. It had been more than a decade since their arrest in the Carpathian Mountains. What a difference those ten years had made in their lives. Those two naive English travelers had become authors, fundraisers, benefactresses, and promoters of education; confident women who had overcome tremendous obstacles in order to accomplish their goal. As they heard the sultan's words read, surrounded by Bosnian elite, they must have felt a sense of satisfaction. They could now return home knowing that the deaconesses would continue their work in Sarajevo. From England they could continue to raise money, direct school policy, hire and pay teachers, all while maintaining the life of travel and privilege they had always enjoyed. Their presence in Sarajevo, apart from periodic visits to inspect the school, was not necessary, and they preferred not to be restricted by the day-to-day tasks of running an educational institution. They were advisors and benefactresses. It was the perfect combination of a meaningful *and* comfortable existence. But comfort and purpose rarely go together, as circumstances would soon prove.

In January 1870 the school opened its doors. However, before the end of two years, the deaconesses had returned to

Germany, and the school was empty. A couple of Orthodox girls had attended when the school first opened, until a sermon was preached in the Orthodox Church against the deaconesses and their work. Other harmful rumors spread throughout town: the school was a clandestine attempt to export Bosnian children to foreign countries; the deaconesses were sent to denationalize and Germanize the innocent students; the goal was not education, but proselytizing. After two months, only two Roman Catholic girls from Dalmatia remained enrolled. A report from the British and Foreign Bible Society in 1870 explained:

> The population of Sarajevo is strongly inimical to every species of religious reformation . . .
> Some recent endeavors to establish a girls' school, somewhat worthy of that name, in which education based on Bible teaching should be given, has aroused a tempest of indignation against the intruders who have ventured on so bold a step.[32]

Surprisingly, the opposition was not coming from the Turkish government or Osmanli officials who were accustomed to the presence of English and American missionaries and viewed the little school as below their interest. It was the Orthodox and Catholic population who, after surviving almost four hundred years under the rule of a larger, stronger, foreign power, were slow to believe that some sinister motivation did not lie beneath the English ladies' altruistic charity.

What use was an educational institution without teachers or students?

Adeline and Georgina had once noted to Katerina Simitić,

the schoolmistress from Ipek, that it takes courage and cleverness to start a school. Adeline would need both, and more, for the girls' school to succeed. Pastor Fliedner sent word to Adeline and Georgina in England that his confidence in their project had dissipated and he was removing the deaconesses from such a hostile and unrewarding environment. Immediately, Adeline made preparations for the trip to Sarajevo. However, for the first time since she and Georgina began traveling in Europe fifteen years earlier, she made the journey alone.

Georgina, whose health had never been strong, had not recovered from the three years of exhausting travel through the Balkans: the shortage of nutritional food, the bouts of fever, the extended exposure to the sun. She was in no condition to make another long trek to Bosnia, much less contribute to the direction of a school. Their lives were diverging. In November 1871 Georgina, desiring a quieter life, married Sir Charles Seabright and moved to the island of Corfu, where he served as the English Consul General for the Ionian Islands. As Georgina prepared for her wedding day, Adeline was making the slow transition from West to East—Paris, Vienna, Prague, Agram (Zagreb), Sisak—each leg of the trip taking her farther from her world of comfort and deeper into this culture she knew, but could not understand. The stark transition from Austrian Brod to Turkish Brod on the border of Bosnia would have only heightened Georgina's absence. Adeline was left to face the prospect of complete failure in Sarajevo without the aid of her friend, editor, "aunt", travel companion, and like-minded confidant who had been, for most of her adult life, closer to her than family. Their complementary personalities had allowed them to do what they could not have done individually. Without Adeline's courage, perhaps Georgina would not have found adventure and purpose outside of the safety and comfort of Europe. On the other hand, Adeline may not have survived for long without Georgina's common sense. Now Adeline was alone, enduring the last one hundred and forty miles from the border in a springless cart, the unavoidable complications before her, the recent failures behind her, and no one beside her. Yet, she made the trip. She was determined to find a door, a key, a path to success. For the sake of the school, the girls, and the people of Bosnia.

As she crested the last peak, Adeline saw the beautiful and complicated city of Sarajevo, with her one hundred and fifty white stone minarets standing boldly against the green hills. She was, at the same time, glorious, like a rose bush sprinkled with dew, and dangerous, like that very same bush, thorns hidden beneath scarlet petals, in the hands of the careless.

WHAT THEY ARE MADE OF

1871-1875

*We will wait for that beautiful day when we will see who the
real missionaries are and what they are made of.*
—Adeline Paulina Irby[33]

*The longer I live, the more I am certain that the great difference
between men, between the feeble and the powerful, the great
and the insignificant, is energy—invincible determination—a
purpose once fixed and then death or victory. That quality will
do anything that can be done in this world; and no talents, no
circumstances, no opportunities, will make a two-legged
creature a man without it.*
—Sir Thomas Fowell Buxton[34]

WHEN ADELINE ARRIVED in Sarajevo in 1871 to take over
the school from the deaconesses, she went straight to

work. For the institution to succeed, she needed to convince community and religious leaders, as well as the parents, that she was not working to further some political, ethnic, or otherwise divisive cause. She was laboring for the welfare of the Bosnian people. But the people's skepticism was understandable. What were they to do with this Protestant English woman? What box could they fit her in or category of understanding could they file her under? How could this city of mahalas (neighbourhoods where life was divided by religion and nationality, and resources were used to protect and maintain that identity) comprehend this strange woman who was using her resources for the good of those outside her group? The only possible answer in the minds of most Sarajevans was that she was building her own little Protestant *mahala*.

One of her first changes was to remove the golden cross that the German deaconesses had installed on the roof. She knew the cross was a powerful symbol. In Slovakia, she had noted the adoration shown by traveling peasants towards the life-size crucifixes along the road and the comfort they received knowing that the one they worshipped understood what it meant to suffer. Yet she realized that that very same symbol which brought comfort could cause misunderstanding. Adeline was more committed to the meaning of the cross than the symbol, the sacrifice of self rather than the mere representation of it. The school was meant to be a place of refuge, growth and education for all who entered. She preferred that the exterior of the schoolhouse be bare, if that meant that the inside would be decorated with bright-faced Bosnian children.

Adeline's school had at least one unplanned positive result. According to the British Consul Holmes, writing in

January 1873, "The English Protestant school . . . has given rise to a considerable effort on the part of both the Greeks [i.e. Orthodox] and Catholics to provide education for their children in schools of their own, which are now kept up with much more efficiency than formerly. The teachers are superior to what they were, and the attendance larger and more regular." He continued to write that the philanthropic effort of Miss Irby and Miss Mackenzie had successfully "stimulated this people . . . to advance in the right direction, and improve the means of education."[35]

One might imagine that this competition would have frustrated Adeline, but, instead, she was delighted to advance the cause of education whether directly or indirectly. At the time, she had two Roman Catholic girls in her school, so she and Staka Skenderova, an Orthodox woman who had come alongside to help run the school, paid a visit to one of the new institutions. She later described the incident:

> *When the school of the nuns was opened I sent to them, much to their astonishment, the only two Roman Catholic children who were in our house. I shall never forget the horror of the good nuns when, accompanied by Halgia Staka, I first paid them a visit. The sight of two heretics, a native schismatic and the very Protestant whose influence they had come to counteract, was too much for them; they fell to crossing themselves in pious fear. We were afterwards on friendly terms, and exchanged various good offices.*[36]

It did not matter to her where or by whom the girls were

educated, only that they received the opportunity to learn and contribute to their families and society. She hoped that, one day, her work educating the poorest Bosnians would even provoke the wealthier Muslim society to move their girls into schools where they could learn to read and write. Her agenda was strikingly open and liberal for that period of time: free room, board, and education for all who enrolled, regardless of religion or nationality.

Adeline's persistence, and the character her presence showed, eventually paid off. After a few years, more children had been brought in than seemed reasonable for them to take; but the continuing success of the school required her full attention—convincing parents, correcting rumors, persuading community leaders and averting collapse. She was not alone in this work. Staka, a dependable and industrious Serbian woman who ran the only other girls' school in Bosnia, worked alongside her. Mrs. Tabory, the wife of the Bosnian representative of the British and Foreign Bible Society, was the institution's matron, caring for the boarding students. In addition to that, starting in the fall of 1872, the schoolhouse welcomed a new British ex-patriot, Priscilla Johnston.

Priscilla spent most of her life before 1872 on a large estate, Northrepps Hall, 35 miles to the northeast of Adeline's family home. When, at the age of ten, her mother died, she and her five siblings moved there to live with their widowed grandmother, Hannah Buxton. Life at Northrepps had a balance of purpose and fun. During holidays, the house overflowed with family, spilling out onto the large lawn where cockatoos roamed, the music and laughter drifting across the fields where horses, dogs and cats watched the revelers with curiosity. With two brothers and three sisters, an enormous extended family, and the assorted possibilities of the country estate, Priscilla's childhood was cheery and full. However, as she grew older and her siblings married and moved away, her life became restricted by the daily needs of Lady Buxton. She was her grandmother's constant companion and caretaker. Although she may have wanted to travel, to see the world like other gentlewomen of her age and financial station, she was not necessarily disappointed by her position and assignment. Through Lady Buxton she was connected to the rich and meaningful heritage of her family.

Lady Buxton's husband, Sir Thomas Fowell Buxton, became an MP in the British House of Commons in 1825, taking the seat William Wilberforce left vacant at his retirement. Sir Thomas did more than fill Wilberforce's space, he carried forward the flag that Wilberforce had born since 1788: the abolition of slavery. Perhaps no two men did more to end the inhumane system of the African slave trade than William Wilberforce and Sir Thomas Buxton. What Wilberforce started and pursued his entire career, Buxton finished, with the passing of the Slavery Abolition Act in 1833, effectively outlawing slavery in Britain and its territories.

Lady Buxton's sister, Elizabeth Fry, also left a significant influence on the world. At the beginning of the nineteenth century, she worked tirelessly to bring reform to the British prison system, which was overcrowded and in disrepair. She was known to invite nobles to spend the night with her in a cell in order to draw attention to the inhumane conditions. Because of her efforts, new legislation was passed to improve the treatment of prisoners and she became known as 'The Angel of the Prisons'. She believed that every woman was called upon for a time to leave her family and devote herself to a noble cause.

Priscilla's family tradition was one of humanitarian work that extended throughout England and around the globe. This philanthropic spirit arose from their deep Christian faith. Within the Anglican Church in the late 18th and early 19th centuries, there was a movement of philanthropic-minded evangelicals* for whom humanitarian work and the spread of the gospel were not mutually exclusive. They were driven by the belief that the truths found in the Bible could not only transform individual lives, but also society; that the grace of Jesus' sacrificial death given to believers to meet their deepest needs should motivate those same believers to graciously and sacrificially give themselves to meet the needs of others; that Jesus' resurrection from the dead brought not only spiritual life to believers, but also the ability to live better and different lives.

William Wilberforce and Sir Buxton were at the center of this movement. In his book published in 1789, Wilberforce encourages the reader to "cast yourselves then on [God's] undeserved mercy; he is full of love, and will not spurn you: surrender yourselves into his hands, and solemnly resolve, through his Grace, to dedicate henceforth all your faculties and powers to his service."[37] Faith and service were intertwined. Sir Buxton, only days before the session of Parliament which would signify the commencement of his antislavery

---

* The label evangelical has had various meanings throughout the history of Christianity. It derives from the Greek word meaning "good news" or "gospel."

career, wrote in his journal: "Grant, O Lord God . . . that I may choose for my first objects those which merit the dedication of all my powers, possessions, energies, and influence... the salvation of my own soul and the service of God, promoting the salvation of others and their welfare."[38] He continued to ask God for strength to be consistent and serious in prayer and to resist temptation, but also to end slavery and reform the prisons. To him, all his work for others flowed out of his faith in God.

Priscilla must have sat with Lady Buxton for hours listening to family stories, discussing philanthropic endeavors around the world, talking about God, and planning what she might do one day when she too had the opportunity to serve. When that time came, with the death of her grandmother in 1872, she was ready to follow the legacy laid out for her. She would join Adeline Irby and her work in Bosnia.

After a few years, Adeline and Priscilla established a consistent rhythm for their work in Sarajevo: leave England in August; remain in Bosnia until May; return home for the summer to rest, avoid the harsh Sarajevo heat, raise money for the school, and enjoy the comfort of family and friends. In 1875, though, they changed that pattern, leaving in late July in order to spend some time traveling through Bosnia recruiting children for their school. If they had not left early, perhaps they would have never reached Sarajevo.

Their first warning came in Vienna from a Serbian source, an adjutant of the Prince of Serbia, who urged them not to venture into Bosnia because of a potential uprising of the

Bosnian Christian peasants. A Hungarian doctor who was returning to the Turkish cavalry unit in which he served echoed this exhortation on a Sava River steamer. His opinion, based on what he had seen in his extensive time in the country, was that the rising would be as deep and widespread as the causes; things would soon be terribly serious. Despite these signs, the ladies were paddled across the Sava in a canoe—nothing more than a hollowed out tree—and continued as planned through Gradiška and on to Banja Luka. Along the way, they noted that the stretch of railway from Banja Luka had been wholly destroyed, the bridges pulled down and the rails pulled up. After a short visit in Banja Luka with a merchant's family whose nervous behavior only confirmed what they had learned so far, they returned to the Austrian side of the border. On Sunday August 15th, the day after they left Banja Luka, the uprising broke out in northern Bosnia.

Undeterred, Adeline and Priscilla took the steamer from Gradiška to Brod, planning to continue on to Sarajevo. On board they met a Croatian lawyer who was returning home to Brod. He told them that from the deck of the boat that same morning, not far from Gradiška, he had seen women and children hiding in the bushes at the water's edge and peasants running about in a panic with hoes and spades in their hands. An acquaintance of the ladies, Vaso Vidević, a Bosnian merchant and eventual supporter of the insurgent peasants, brought them into the cabin of the ship and, "pale as death" and with tears in his eyes, entreated them not to go on to Sarajevo.

"The disturbance will spread eastward towards Brod and the Austrian post-cart is likely to be fired upon. It is too dangerous! Please don't go," he implored.

The ladies, retaining their sense of humor, replied encouragingly, "It might prove a good thing for your cause if two English ladies were killed."

"Yes, that's true," he agreed, "but not you!"

The ladies went anyway.

They left Turkish Brod on August 17 on the post-cart and traveled through the night, stopping only at Kiseljak the second night, reaching Sarajevo on the 19th. The ladies found the city in a panic. The Christian inhabitants were either preparing to flee or boarding themselves up in their homes, fearing that the disturbance would soon reach Sarajevo. Several of the leading Christian merchants appeared at the ladies' school, begging shelter if the expected butchery commenced. The Austrian consul and his wife had already left. Adeline and Priscilla quickly formed a plan to evacuate the school.

Four days after their arrival, the ladies were in a convoy of four carts carrying five students, two teachers and a maid, leaving Sarajevo for the Austrian border. At Brod, they saw the signs of war: bodies drifting with the dark currents of the Sava or cast up on a sand island nearby; crowds of Bosnians filling the Turkish side of the border, clamoring to cross the last watery distance into the safety of Slavonia. The pupils, who had been hastily dressed in western clothes in order to avoid the scrutiny of the border guards, were on their way to Prague where they would be enrolled in the Bohemian Higher Girls' School to advance their education. Adeline and Priscilla were returning to London to determine what to do next.

* * *

By December, they had developed a plan to work among the refugees who were fleeing Bosnia. They published letters in *The Times* of London requesting donations and raised a significant amount of money. The work, however, was in jeopardy. Adeline was having second thoughts about returning and delayed their departure. She was staying at a friend's country estate in Derbyshire, assisting her with the care of her elderly parents. The longer she stayed and the more useful she felt, the more reluctant she became to leave those comforts for the refugee camps of Slavonia. Perhaps she should wait out the war in England and then resume her work at the school when it concluded. She had already given a third of her life to the South Slavs, could this be the time to transition to another season of life? The horrors of war and the warnings of concerned associates had failed to keep her out of Bosnia, but now the comforts of England were succeeding. She had long before accepted the value of being, as she said of Katerina Simitic, "a woman whose mind had thus grasped the idea of self-devotion for the general good," but now she wrestled with the cost that kind of life demands.

Yet, in that house, lived the one person who could speak authoritatively into Adeline's life: Florence Nightingale. Florence, whom she met in 1869, was one of Adeline's friends, but also one of her heroes. As a young woman she had admired Florence's courageous work during the Crimean War, caring for wounded and dying soldiers, and her efforts to modernize the nursing profession afterwards. She counted it an honor to be in the presence of such a renowned woman, to listen to her stories and to learn from her experiences. Who would want to leave the comforts of Lea Hurst, the Nightingale country estate, for the refugee camps of Slavonia?

To Florence, though, even a second's pause or a delayed step was unacceptable for someone seeking to serve God and others. She once said of her work in Crimea, "I have done my duty. I have identified my fate with that of the heroic dead. It has been a great cause." It was time, she told Adeline, for her to do her duty; she had made a commitment to the people who had given to her cause and turning back was not an option; the Bosnian refugees needed her help. It was time for Adeline to identify her fate and discover what she was really made of.

THE PROFESSOR
AND THE PRIEST

*History is not holy because it is full of lies, as are the people
who write it.*
—Adeline Paulina Irby[39]

O N A BEAUTIFUL, sunny April day, during our first year
in Sarajevo, I was showing a guest around the city when
he made a suggestion that changed the next year of my life. It
was Bill's first visit to Bosnia so we were making the most of
his time: up the hill to the lookout at Vratnik, down the valley
to my favorite coffee shops in Baščaršija, along the Miljacka to
the important historical bridges. As we walked, I began telling him about Adeline and her work in Sarajevo. That week, a
two-page article had been published in the *Oslobođenje* newspaper about her life. He was asking so many questions that I
decided to give him an impromptu "Miss Irby tour". I showed
him *Misirbina* street, the green and white road sign, the location of her school, and the museum where some of her jewelry was displayed, all the while telling him Adeline's story.
When we finally sat down to dinner, Bill was more excited

than I was.

"You have to write a book about her life," Bill said after we placed our order.

"What do you mean?"

"Miss Irby's story needs to be told. The kind of life she lived, the choices she made, the way she treated people. People need to know about her."

I was more skeptical than Bill. "You realize that I am an engineer by training, right? What place do I have writing a book?"

"Well," Bill responded, "I do believe that you are the only other Irby living in Bosnia."

"Yes, but we are just getting settled in and I still have a long way to go on learning the language. It doesn't seem like the best timing for writing a book."

"Ok, alright," Bill relented. "I just think you should consider it."

A couple days later Bill left, but his suggestion didn't. The following week I was reading back through the newspaper article when I noticed the date of Adeline's death, September 15, 1911. It struck me that the one-hundredth anniversary of her death was eighteen months away. What better opportunity could there be to talk about her life than the centennial of her death? Perhaps it was the right time to write a book.

I pulled out a piece of paper and a pen and started making a list. At the top of the page I wrote, "Learn how to write a book." For a few seconds I stared at the sentence I had written. I changed the period to an exclamation point: "Learn to write a book!" If I was writing a book, I should know how to do it. Next on the list I added, "Collect everything written by or about Adeline." That would take a while, I knew, but it was a necessary key to understanding what she did. On the next line I wrote, "Understand Bosnian history." It was, perhaps, the most daunting task. After reading numerous books on Balkan history I had not yet accomplished it. I would need to find help.

Sitting back, I read over my list. Something was missing. If I did all three I could write a good history book full of facts and figures describing Adeline's work, but would I really understand Adeline? She was more than the places she visited and people she helped. She was a person. What use would it be to know what she did if the understanding went no deeper?

At the bottom of the page I wrote in capital letters: "WHY?" That was the key question I needed to answer. Why did Adeline do what she did? Solving that mystery could prove as difficult as unraveling the history of Bosnia.

"History is *sehara*," the professor began, referring to the decorative wooden boxes made by traditional craftsmen in Bosnia and Hercegovina, "people reach in and take out whatever they want."

The history professor and I were discussing Miss Irby in his office at the University of Sarajevo; he sat comfortably at his desk, half-hidden by stacks of books. We met, by happenstance, the week before when I wandered onto the university campus in search of an expert to help me understand the history behind Adeline's story.

"During every major transition or war in Bosnia, people have reached into the sehara and used history as justification and motivation for their cause," the professor continued. "That is why, when you are trying to understand the history of this country, it is important to interpret the person in their own context."

"Well," I replied, "now you understand the problem I have. I am an American man trying to understand an English woman who traveled in Bosnia and Hercegovina over a century ago."

"Yes," he said laughing, "that is the challenge of historiography."

"What was the context that Miss Irby entered into?"

"They were turbulent times. At the end of the 19th century, everything was changing: there was a multiplication of national movements, the end of four centuries of Ottoman control, a shift from east to west, a transition from a Muslim state to a Christian state. It was the beginning of the modern history of Bosnia." He paused. "That is why the 19th century is the most important period of history in this country." He smiled to indicate that he, a professor of 19th century Bosnian history, recognized the humor of that statement. "Even then, there was widespread misunderstanding of life in the Balkans. You can pick up two books written at that time and get two completely different pictures of the situation. Especially in England."

"One thing I appreciate about Miss Irby," I added, "was that she tried to understand. I can relate to the challenge she faced as an outsider looking in. But she tried to overcome that obstacle by talking with people in their homes and getting her information directly from the source. I think she tried to be fair."

"I agree," the professor replied, "she tried to understand

and she tried to be fair. She was really brave to try and help the lower class, to lift them up with education, especially with her work for women. In many ways, she was a symbol of the times, a symbol of the change in Bosnia, a symbol of the beginning of Bosnia's modern history, for good or for bad."

"For good or for bad," I repeated. "It seems that different people have varying perspectives on what was good and what was bad in history, and that those perspectives are constantly changing."

"Yes," the professor answered. "For the past five years I have assigned my students the same project, sort of an informal survey. They are required to interview a cross-section of the population—people of all ages, religions, and social stations—asking them one question: Who was better, the Ottoman sultan or the Austro-Hungarian czar? This is not, of course, scientific, but it does provide a yearly snapshot of opinions in Sarajevo. When I started this, the majority of respondents preferred the sultan. But, in the last few years, as Bosnia and Hercegovina has moved towards the west, towards membership in the European Union, the results have shifted. Now, more people prefer the czar."

"I am glad you told me that," I said, "because, as an outsider, I sometimes have trouble keeping up with who is the bad guy in Bosnian history."

The professor chuckled from behind his desk.

I continued, "You know, in the movies from my childhood, the bad guys always wear black and the good guys wear white. That way it's clear who to cheer for. It is not like that in history."

I took a moment to process what I was learning.

"I think that Adeline had a different approach to the world,"

I mused aloud. "Rather than labeling a person or people good or bad, she worked from an internal sense of right and wrong. There were certain things that were right—freedom to worship, freedom to improve oneself, freedom in general. When she saw those good things obstructed, she called it wrong. In doing so, she found herself caught up in the political storm of that generation. But she wasn't driven by politics. She was driven by a desire to help."

"That is why you need to speak about her in her time and not ours," the professor advised. "She was brave; she was really brave. She saw that women needed help and she helped them. Whether it was the right way or not is another question. But she thought it was the right way. And in her work to lift the lower classes and to secure more rights for women according to the European understanding, she became a symbol of the times.

"But don't forget," the professor concluded, "that history is sehara. Even the most positive person can be used for some negative cause."

Not long after my conversation with the professor, I had an opportunity to test out his informal survey. I was returning to Sarajevo from the Croatian coast along a route Adeline traveled one hundred fifty years earlier. She made the journey jostling about in a springless cart, exposed to the elements, in touch with her surroundings. I reclined in a cushioned bus seat, warm despite the cold weather outside, listening to music on my iPod. However, despite modern comforts, travel still has its inherent difficulties.

By the time we passed Mostar, I was the last passenger on the bus. As the driver and I headed into the mountains from Jablanica, the bus began to shake and slow, the driver shifting from fourth, to third, to first, the bus refusing to make the ascent. At last we pulled over onto the side of the road and the driver began to utilize the full breadth of his language. I had been gone a week and was rushing to get home to my family, so the sight of the driver with a toolbox was disheartening. After half an hour of the clinks and clanks of metal on metal, we set off again, but the front door would not close. As the breeze blew in from outside I imagined the wind Adeline must have endured on her journeys.

The driver, eventually deciding that his boss would not approve of his making the last hour of our trip with the door open, pulled off at a restaurant and began making phone calls. He was speaking quickly and angrily so I was not able to make out everything he said, but on each call, he mentioned my name: "The bus broke down and I am stuck here with this *stranac* (foreigner, stranger)", "What am I going to do with this *stranac*?", "This *stranac* needs to get to Sarajevo". Eventually, he called me out of the bus, opened up the baggage compartment, and gestured to my things. I had a medium size travel bag and a small pink bicycle that my friend in Split had given me for my daughter. As I was removing my stuff from the bus, the bus driver began to flag down passing cars. When one would stop, he would walk over to the car, say something unintelligible to the driver and then, midsentence, turn his face towards me and gesture to where I was standing beside the highway, bag in hand and pink bicycle at my side. I eventually realized that he was trying to help me hitchhike the rest of the way to Sarajevo.

At last a man agreed to take me. He was a large, older man, still strong and active, but past middle age. His car was clean and comfortable but he had a washing machine drum sitting on his backseat that made an unbearably loud noise when we rounded curves. To make the situation less awkward, I tried to make conversation, but his answers were short and deep-voiced, almost like a growl. Although he wasn't talkative, he seemed nice enough.

After forty-five minutes I found a topic that he would talk about: Bosnia. We discussed the fact that he had lived in Sarajevo for almost forty years; I told him that I planned to live there for a while. He asked if I liked Bosnia; I told him I did. Bosnia has everything, he told me, trees, water, and natural beauty. Bosnian water could quench the thirst of the world, he said emphatically.

The conversation was going better, so I decided to test out the professor's question. I asked who he thought was better for Bosnia: the Ottoman sultan or the Austrian emperor. He thought for a second. He then said that he had no idea. He told me that he hadn't personally met either one so he couldn't say. The thing about the past, he said, is that it has already passed.

Silence.

For the rest of the drive, except for the occasional clanging of the washing machine drum, I was left to my thoughts. *What am I doing writing a book about Bosnian history? People in Bosnia have already lived through history once. Why make them live through it again? Is it worth the trouble and confusion to tell Adeline's story?*

★   ★   ★

A couple weeks after the adventure with the broken bus, I was in a different office across town from the philosophy faculty discussing Miss Irby. The sitting room was much larger than the professor's office, decorated with antique furniture and oil paintings. The adjacent room was a reading library with floor to ceiling bookshelves containing worn hardback manuscripts. I sat nervously on the yellow upholstered couch waiting for the Orthodox priest, who was in the kitchen preparing coffee for us. I had seen his picture in the newspaper *Oslobođenje* as part of an article about Adeline; he was standing beside her grave. After a few failed attempts to get an appointment, I was sitting in his office.

"Thanks for taking the time for us to talk," I opened the conversation as he set our espressos on the coffee table. "I have been researching the life of Miss Irby—reading the books she wrote as well as books written about her—in order to write her story. What can you tell me about her?"

"She was a great woman," the priest began, crossing his legs in his antique armchair. He was fairly young for a priest, dressed in modern clothes, yet somehow seemed to match his more traditional surroundings. "In her time, it was popular for women to travel. But when she came to this region, it was a turning point for her. I think that she was greatly moved by the suffering of the people and realized that education was not developed enough. In some way, she became bound with the people here. I believe, especially, bound to the Serbian people—maybe you won't agree."

"I think that she came here looking for people who needed help," I replied, "and helped those she found."

"She was a humanitarian her whole life," the priest continued, "and did not classify herself by choosing sides.

Sometimes she would focus her energy here, other times there, however she thought was most fitting. But, she was still more connected to the Orthodox of Bosnia. Because of that you won't find a lot about Miss Irby in Bosnia. The average citizen of Sarajevo doesn't know anything about her."

"Most people I've talked to think she was a nurse," I agreed about the lack of information.

The priest proceeded, "Today's official politics avoid talking about people who were more bound to one nation than another, but the fact is, she wasn't bound to anyone. She only helped those who, at the time, needed help."

"That is why I am writing a book about her. Her story is one that people should know—the way she lived her life to help others."

"In the Balkans," the priest interjected, "you have to be careful because everything you do can be twisted. Everything is divided here. The Serbs will say, 'Oh, he's writing a book about Miss Irby; that's wonderful. He's "ours".' Muslims will say, 'He was probably paid by Serbs to write the book.' And the Croatians will hang in the back and not supply you with any valid commentary. What I want to say is that, living here, many things become schizophrenic. It's either black or white. It's hard to explain to someone that you are talking about something that doesn't fit into the categories."

"No, she doesn't fit the categories," I said. "Because of that, her story has the potential to bring people together."

"Of course, the life of a person like Miss Irby can't be a reason for dividing people, but uniting them. So you need to work to understand the historical events in her time and write a book that represents her work and that she would be proud of."

The priest's reference to her work reminded me of the conversation with the professor and our discussion on Adeline as a symbol of modern Bosnia. I asked the priest the same question, "What do you think Miss Irby symbolizes? What is she a symbol of?"

"She symbolizes that which does not exist anymore: kindness, honesty, strength; character that lives for others; that greatest virtue, to lay your life down for someone else. She lived like she was responsible for the world and for mankind. What she did rose above human nature and egoism and moved towards something that is from another world, God's world... That is what she symbolizes for me."

As I descended the stairs from his office, I thought about this sehara, history, full of complicated and often contradictory facts and dates, this chest from which both good and evil men draw their weapons. "This is the challenge of historiography," I heard the professor say. At that moment, I began to doubt that it was a challenge worth facing. "The thing about the past is that it has already passed," I heard the man from the car ride say. At that moment, I was not sure that the past should be relived.

"Then I remembered something else," the professor said.

We were discussing Adeline's legacy and how the perception of her work had changed since her death. He told me that certain people had used Adeline's words during the past century to promote their political movements and advance their agenda. People had drawn her words out of the sehara for their own purposes.

"Maybe it is not a good idea to write about her," I responded.

"Listen," he replied, "Miss Irby came to help without any expectation of getting something in return. If Miss Irby motivates us to be better in this world, than that is reason enough to write a book about her."

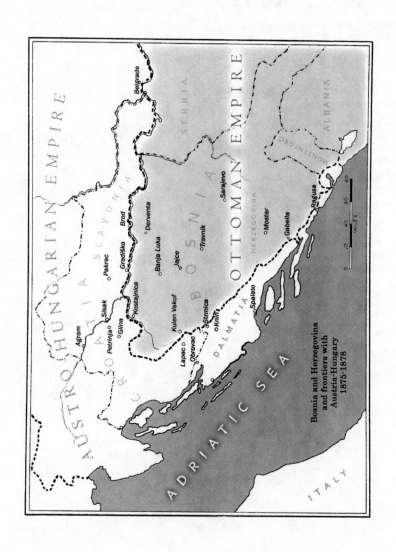

Bosnia and Herzegovina
and frontiers with
Austria-Hungary
1875-1878

REFUGEE WORK BEGINS

1876

> *Other refuge have I none,*
> *Hangs my helpless soul on Thee;*
> *Leave, ah! leave me not alone,*
> *Still support and comfort me.*
> *All my trust on Thee is stayed,*
> *All my help from Thee I bring;*
> *Cover my defenseless head*
> *With the shadow of Thy wing.*
> —From the song "Jesus, Lover of my Soul", sung in
> Adeline's school

THE SMALL AND relatively unimportant district of Nevesinje in Hercegovina, twenty-five miles to the east of Mostar, was the match that set the Balkans on fire the summer of 1875. The majority of villagers were farmers whose livelihood depended on what they drew out of the soil of *Nevesinsko Polje*, a large, dried up lake bed surrounded by a rocky, limestone wasteland. During the best of years, the land produced just enough to satisfy the government tax collectors, the landowner, and the worker's family. But in 1874, the crops failed. The year's small harvest could not legally be gathered until it was assessed by the government auditors, but the inspectors did not appear and the crops rotted in the field. It was not until January 1875 that the tax collectors arrived and, desiring to squeeze out every last penny, over-valued the yield, leaving the peasants with an impossibly exorbitant charge, which they, out of necessity, refused to pay. Seeking to collect their demands by force, the government officials instigated an escalating cycle of violence from which the farmers retreated into the surrounding hills.

What started as a wholly agrarian revolt against the taxation system quickly evolved, with the help of political opportunists, into a full-fledged insurrection. The peasant farmers were the primary victims. Fleeing the destruction, they received a new name: refugees. As the uprising spread into northern Bosnia, neighboring countries were flooded with huddled masses of the displaced: 50,000 in Montenegro, 30,000 in Dalmatia, 25,000 in Serbia, and 40,000 in Croatia. Petar Uzelac, an eyewitness, reported:

> *What a scene of wretchedness! Hundreds and hundreds dragging themselves along the dusty road— men, women, and children . . . Weary women and little children can scarcely crawl along; some of the sick (for the most part smallpox cases) fall down by the way. I go up to a group which is gathering round some object on the road-side; a woman has been overtaken by the pains of labor and,*

surrounded by her children, is giving birth to an infant. A few steps further on is another group: here lies in the last agony a woman who has been wounded; seven wounds on her body . . . Many sink down on the dusty hard roadside . . . Fathers of families go to seek bread in the village. Some have brought away a few coins, and can pay for it. Now, a father returns with some bread, which he divides among his family; the children watch every mouthful with longing eyes. Another father returns empty-handed; a cry of distress bursts forth. Alas! there are hundreds upon hundreds of such scenes; for fresh bands of fugitives are crossing daily at one or another point on the frontier into Austrian territory.[40]

The flight of the Bosnian peasants (one-sixth of the total Christian population that first summer) took its toll: "the father loses the son, the mother the daughter; the young and the feeble perish on the way; weeks or months go by before the scattered members of a family find one another, and the fate of many is never known. No property, hardly the bare life, can be saved."[41] With winter fast approaching and the refugees receiving barely enough subsidies from the Austrian government to buy bread, the crisis was only beginning.

In England, not many knew about the uprising and the conservative government downplayed those stories that were made public. But on November 16, an advertisement appeared in the *The Times* requesting funds for The Bosnian and Herzegovinian Orphan Relief Fund. According to a pamphlet they distributed, the fund was meant for "housing,

feeding, and training as many as possible of the refugee children; boarding them out to families; establishing small orphan homes; finding work for the mothers." The members
of the board included various leaders of the Anglican church
and philanthropically minded members of the nobility. The
first donator to the fund was Miss Florence Nightingale, at
£50. The directresses were Miss Priscilla Johnston and Miss
Adeline Paulina Irby.

When Adeline and Priscilla arrived in Slavonia in January
1876, they knew what they wanted to do, but had no idea how
to go about doing it. How do you start schools among refugees who don't even have food to eat or clothes to wear? The
families were already frightened. How could they trust their
children to two English women whose homeland supported
the empire they were fighting against? Added to those complications was the ongoing war. They quickly discovered that
many of the relief efforts were far more interested in supporting the insurgents than helping the refugees; money meant
for blankets and food went to purchasing weapons, medicine given for the sick civilians used for injured soldiers. They
were determined (and Miss Nightingale was adamant on this)
to avoid politics so they could best provide relief, but, in the
Balkans at the time, even the air was political. Who could
they trust?

The first few weeks they traveled through Slavonia (Sisak,
Petrinja, Glina, Kostajnica) visiting camps and observing
the condition of the refugees. Meanwhile, Miss Nightingale,
who had volunteered to manage the fund from England, was

impatiently wondering why she wasn't receiving word that schools were being formed. Obviously, Florence, who had never been to the Balkans, did not understand the complicated position in which the ladies found themselves. Adeline and Priscilla had money, that is sure, but they did not have a building, teachers, students, the trust of the refugees, or permission from the Austrian authorities. By the end of January, not a single orphan was housed nor a single child educated. Add to that, very little money had been distributed. The ladies' plan was beginning to seem naive and superficial, especially to someone as organized and calculating as Florence. In their defense, they did not waste any of the funds they had collected, but rather saved it for the time when it could be best used. Also, their strategy took longer to enact because it required national Bosnian help. If the ladies had quickly started a school, administered it and taught the classes themselves, they would have seen results immediately, but their success would have been limited. They could only be in one place at a time. Instead, they spent the first months in Slavonia building relationships with community leaders and teachers, a decision that would later prove optimal.

At the beginning of March they found the opportunity they were waiting for. While inquiring from some travelers about the condition of Bosnian refugees in their villages, one elderly man mentioned that there was a young crippled man living in his hut who, he believed, had been a teacher in Bosnia before the uprising. Adeline's description of the man upon meeting him was that "a more desponding, haggard-looking object I scarcely ever saw."[42] The ladies had him read and write in front of them and quickly discovered him to be, in spite of his appearance, bright and intelligent.

Wasting no time, the following day they drove out to the village of Kukunjevac, in which they found an old abandoned school building that would meet their needs and lodging for their newest teacher. Within a few days, on March 6, the new school was opened. Adeline had a photograph taken to commemorate the moment: a long line of students, dressed in their newly-made garments stretched across the front of the two-story school building. The young instructor, who had shown himself both skilled and energetic and whose appearance and demeanor had drastically changed after taking the position, stood at the center in a dark colored cloak holding an open book in his hand. An overwhelming sense of peace and progress pervaded the scene.

An article in *The Times* on March 13 reported this first sign of success: a school had been opened with one hundred sixty-one children under the age of twelve led by a local schoolmaster and a second was opening in the town of Pakrac. Both schools were administered by local boards that included professors from the *Preparandija*, the teachers' training school at Pakrac, and the leading Serb merchant in town. Because the schools operated without the ladies' daily involvement, they were free to start others throughout Slavonia. By the end of May, there were seven schools with over three hundred children. All of the students were fed, clothed and vaccinated; eleven girls were boarded out with families; nearly three thousand women and children were provided with shoes and cloth for making garments (one thousand yards of woolen material); one thousand forty blankets were distributed.

The institutions provided security and stability for the children—a sense of home in the midst of refugee life—and central locations for the distribution of aid to the families. The ladies were accomplishing the goals they had set out for the fund and they were doing it for much less money than most of the other relief organizations in the area. They spent freely of their own money, never charging the fund for their own expenses or for the brochures and circulars used to advertise their work. However, by the end of June, the fund needed to be replenished and that would require the work of both ladies back in England. In early July, as Adeline and Priscilla were arriving in London, the conflict in the Balkans was changing (a change that would make their work even harder and leave one-third of the Christian population of Bosnia exiled or homeless). Serbia and Montenegro declared war on Turkey.

Returning to Croatia in October, Adeline was dramatically more confident, organized, and encouraged than just a year before. With the publication across England of Turkish atrocities in Bulgaria, public opinion took a drastic turn away from the long-held pro-Turkish position. As interest increased in the Balkans, Adeline was one of the few whose experience gave her a factual perspective on the conflict. When they had first started The Bosnian and Herzegovinian Fugitive Orphan Relief Fund, much of the money had been raised from their family and friends. As the plight of Balkan refugees received weekly attention from the press, their fund gained broader support. They left London with £3000 in their fund and one hundred bales of clothing that had been donated and collected by women throughout the country.

During the fall of 1876, the ladies, who were now well-funded and had trusted associates like Professor Josić who managed the schools for them while they were away, quickly expanded their work. They doubled the schools from eight to 16. Adeline and Priscilla housed themselves in a hotel in Pakrac which operated as their home, office, and resource library. Every Sunday, the professors from all of the schools would come and report to the directresses, receive payment and encouragement, collect resources and ideas, return books, and retrieve new ones from the "lending library," which was basically the ladies' personal collection. On Thursdays, Pakrac was flooded with refugees from the surrounding region for market day, and Adeline and Priscilla would often spend four hours or more entertaining requests for help. They were careful to ensure that the fund was only used for Bosnians who truly needed their help. One of their assistants, Palija, who could not read or write, developed an ingenious way to identify the refugees with the greatest need while preventing fraud. He made small tally sticks with two interlocking parts and varying numbers of notches which he used during his exploratory trips from village to village. When he found an impoverished family, he picked out a stick with notches equal to their family size and, retaining half for his records, gave them the corresponding half to bring to the distribution location. It was a simple solution that insured the best use of the limited resources.

Their work kept them busy and provided moments of satisfaction. The tailor for the schools, who prepared clothing for many of the children, had been near death when they first met him. After consistent treatment, he recovered to be a productive part of their growing operation. And that operation was to grow again. In December of 1876, they received a letter from the priest of a small village near Knin, in Dalmatia.

He had heard of their work in Slavonia and informed them that there was no current relief work in his region, where, he was certain, the refugees were in worse condition than in the north. He was right.

THE YOUNG MUSLIM

Ko se jednom napije vode s Baščaršije . . .
(Whoever drinks the water from Baščaršija . . .)
—Common saying in Sarajevo

WALKING THROUGH TOWN one day, I couldn't get the priest's comments out of my mind. His words echoed: in Sarajevo everything is divided; people avoid topics connected to one nationality because everything can be twisted. I was especially affected by his prediction that Muslims would assume the Serbs were paying me simply because I was writing about Adeline. I needed to know if that was true.

I was walking alongside Hotel Europe when I came up with a plan. Cutting over to Ferhadija, the main walking street, I headed towards the cobblestones of Baščaršija. As I passed one of the most important mosques in town—Gazi Husrev-beg—I noticed a few men milling about in the courtyard behind the stone gate. I was tempted to enter, clear my throat loudly, and ask, "Excuse me, do I look like I am on the Serb payroll?" Instead, I continued down Ferhadija, leaving the men to their hushed conversation and prayers.

After a hundred yards I found what I was looking for. To my left was a small passageway—an easily overlooked gap in a row of glass-fronted stores and their tourist-oriented wares. Passing through the archway, I walked along a cool, dark hall that opened into an inner courtyard. Tables and chairs were set up throughout the stone yard and a mix of locals and tourists sat sipping Bosnian coffee and enjoying the sun as it filtered through the trees. Apart from the modern dress of the clientele, I felt as if I had stepped back in time one hundred and fifty years. Completing the scene, a market was spread throughout the courtyard containing bright pink and orange pashmina shawls, freshly polished copper crafts, intricately worked wooden furniture, and stacks of oriental rugs.

I left the courtyard and ascended a flight of stairs, the old wood creaking beneath my feet. The building was the oldest remaining *han* (hostel) in Sarajevo, originally built in the late 16th, early 17th century. The upper floors, which wrapped around the courtyard, had been converted into offices. On the first floor, I found the organization I was seeking: *Mladi Muslimani* (the Young Muslims).

Standing in the hallway in front of the door marked *Mladi Muslimani* my heart rate began to increase. I did not know anyone in the organization; I had heard about them once during a tour of the city. The corridor walls were plastered with pictures of former members, including a large section dedicated to Alija Izetbegović, the leader of the Bosnian Muslims during the break-up of Yugoslavia. My plan to walk into the Young Muslims office and ask if someone would talk with me was starting to seem naive. I knocked. Hearing nothing, I pushed on the door and it groaned open.

Behind the door was a medium-sized cafe, empty except

for two guys behind the bar. The one closest to me was standing. He had light, short hair and was wearing an orange t-shirt. The other, who was sitting on the counter, was darker in complexion and wore a beard with no mustache. I quickly crossed the room, feeling awkward beneath their questioning gaze.

"*Zdravo*," I greeted them. Then, continuing in Bosnian, "I would like to speak to a member of the Young Muslims."

The guy in the orange shirt pointed at his friend, who seemed to be in his mid-twenties. "He is a member of the organization. You should talk with him."

Looking at his friend, who did not seem pleased to be volunteered, I asked, "Would you be willing to answer a few questions for me?"

He shrugged his shoulders. "Why not." Then he led me to a table next to an open window looking onto the courtyard below.

Once seated, we proceeded in a mix of Bosnian and English, neither of us completely comfortable in our second language.

"I am Josh. I want to get your opinion on a book I am writing."

"OK. I am Aziz."

"How long have you been a member of *Mladi Muslimani*?"

"I joined seven or eight years ago."

"Are you a student?"

"I was, but I don't have money right now to finish my degree. It is hard to find a job these days. For three years I worked in the Blood Transfusion Institute here in Sarajevo, but there is no pay for a job like that. Maybe one day I can finish."

"Well, the woman I am writing about worked to bring education to Bosnians who couldn't afford it. Do you know the road behind BBI? *Mis Irbina ulica?*"

"Yes, of course."

"I am writing a book about her. Miss Irby."

"Oh," he remarked, suddenly more interested in our conversation, "I have heard of her."

I gave him a brief summary of Miss Irby's life, emphasizing her work to improve education for poor Bosnian girls and the sacrifices she made to help refugees. I explained to him that she offered help to anyone who would accept it, but that the majority of her work was with Bosnian Serbs. "As part of my research for the book, I have been interviewing various people around Sarajevo. The Orthodox priest I spoke with told me that Muslims would not be interested in her story because she is associated with the Serbs. What do you think about that?"

"I disagree with him. I guess it is all about your perspective. I view Sarajevo as one city, like a person made up of different parts. You have Baščaršija, which was built by the Ottomans. That is like one arm." He stretched out his right arm demonstratively. "Then there is the Austro-Hungarian part of town. That is like the other arm." He waved with his left arm. "The modern buildings, maybe they are like the head. Miss Irby, she is a part of that body too." He laid both hands on his chest. "I don't know, maybe even the heart. Everything that has happened here, everyone who has come here, has added to that body. Sarajevo is the sum of all the good and bad things in her history."

"Kind of like a mixed salad," I added. "You have your tomatoes, your cucumber, your lettuce."

"Yes, exactly. I like that about this city. It is a part of me."

We sat in silence for a moment. There was laughter from the café below.

Aziz continued, "You know, I remember walking down Miss Irby Street as a kid. I never knew who it was named for. If you erase that street, it is like cutting off part of the body—like a man without a hand. It just wouldn't be Sarajevo anymore."

"I think you and I agree," I said, "but not everyone shares that perspective."

"I know. Some people think that Sarajevo would be better if all the mosques were destroyed. But that would not be Sarajevo. Others prefer that the Catholic Churches were removed. That would not be Sarajevo. If the synagogues were torn down, if the Orthodox Churches were erased, that would not be Sarajevo. That would not be my city," he concluded, his voice resolute. "Sarajevo welcomes anyone who comes for a positive purpose."

I attempted to summarize his thoughts. "What you are saying is that anyone can belong to Sarajevo as long as they are not trying to destroy it."

Aziz laughed out loud rocking back in his chair and stuck out his fist towards me. "Exactly!" I bumped his fist with mine. Gone was the quieter, more reserved Aziz from earlier.

"I guess that Miss Irby belongs to Sarajevo," I said when the laughter died down. "She came because she wanted to help. The whole discussion about whose she is distracts from the main point: she came and helped. Perhaps, had she come at a different point in Bosnian history, she would have helped a different group. Who knows? The more important question to me is why she helped at all."

"Maybe she drank the water," Aziz ventured.

"What do you mean?"

"We have this saying here: *Ko se jednom napije vode s Baščaršije, taj iz Sarajeva otići ne umije.* It basically means that whoever drinks the water in Baščaršija will always return to Sarajevo."

"I guess I drank the water too."

"By the way," Aziz asked, "what made you write a book about Miss Irby?"

"My last name is also Irby."

Aziz sat perfectly still. At first, I was not sure if he understood me. Then, slowly, a flash of excitement appeared in his eyes.

"Really? Is that why you moved here?"

"No, I was already planning to move when I discovered the connection."

"No way!" he exclaimed. The emphatic Aziz returned. "That is crazy. I guess that means you belong to Sarajevo too!"

"I would love for that to be true."

REFUGEE WORK EXPANDS

1877

I have never witnessed a nobler or simpler example of entire self-devotion to the cause of good. They have voluntarily sacrificed whatever attractions are found in the gilded saloons of London to devote themselves to unceasing and wearying labour.
—William Gladstone, four-time British Prime Minister, on Adeline and Priscilla's work[43]

A REPORTER FOR the *Manchester Guardian* named Arthur Evans (who would later become Sir Arthur Evans, famed English archaeologist) gave one of the clearest and most chilling descriptions of the refugees in Dalmatia, northeast of Knin:

> *We approached the Bosnian frontier by way of the village of Strmica, about which as many as 6,000 refugees are crowded. I . . . shuddered at the*

half-starved swarms as they clamored for a piece of
English blanket to cover their rags; but such misery
as was here I had never in my life seen, nor imag-
ined to exist before. It was pitiable. They thought
we had brought food for them all. They crowded
round us, these pinched haggard faces, these lean
bony frames, scarred by disease and bowed down
with hunger; they followed till it seemed a dread-
ful dance of death. There was one lad of twelve,
as pale and frail as one of the little snowdrops on
our path; we could see that he could not live many
hours—and who could wish him to?—yet to him,
as if for protection, clung another younger child,
whose only clothing was a few rags tied together
and eked out by the long tresses of a woman's hair...
in this village alone over six hundred have died in
the last few months.[44]

During the last days of 1876, Adeline and Priscilla left
Pakrac and headed south to Dalmatia, leaving the sixteen
schools in Slavonia under the care of Professor Josić and
the money for distribution under a committee that included Josić, a trusted resident of Pakrac named Vasilije Marković,
two higher officials, and "a very capable Croatian lady." They
traveled by ferry to Zadar and then, by open cart, completed the final eight-hour leg inland under the constant bite of
the *Bura*, the cold north wind that comes down from the
Dinaric Alps. The Austrian administered town of Knin,
their destination, was strategically important to the ladies because it was near to Hungarian controlled Croatia (to
the north) and the battlezones of Hercegovina (to the east).

From the 10th century fortress that rose above the city, the ladies could look out towards the Dinarite mountains over land that was, at that moment, flooded with frightened and helpless refugees.

The ladies knew what they would find as they headed northeast from Knin. During the fall of 1876, clashes in Hercegovina sent a new flood of refugees across the mountains into Dalmatia and the reports reaching *The Times* in London were devastating: "In many parts of Dalmatia the refugees are altogether without shelter. Without further help, they must live or die how they can upon the hill sides."[45] The prospects for the coming winter had been even worse: "I estimate that half of the children who came into Dalmatia died last winter and summer. They have had little shelter, many have had none... This winter the ragged of last year will be naked; the then starving will be dead, and others starving in their place."[46] Now Adeline and Priscilla were going to see for themselves.

On January 15 they journeyed out to the small town of Strmica where the uprising had increased the population tenfold, and quickly began distributing what provisions they had. Setting up in a small shed on a large yard with high walls, they were immediately surrounded by three thousand Bosnians, pressing against the gate, climbing to the top of the walls and onto the roof of the shed, filling the courtyard. Adeline and Priscilla, overwhelmed with the demand, had only enough shirts and bread for the children. With the assistance of four stout helpers they established order and the children began filing in one-by-one, frail arms reaching up to the window of the shed, protein deficient bellies protuberating under rags, pus-filled sores of smallpox covering sad faces, baby teeth chattering against the *Bura*. Priscilla later wrote to her brother that the image was "impossible to describe and impossible to forget."[47] For four hours they gave out food and clothing, writing down the names of each of the six hundred children, until they were certain they could do no more. At that moment, a great shout rose up and a new rabble arrived—more mothers, more babies, more sick and hungry children—begging for any kind of help. They had traveled a great distance having heard that there was food. The ladies continued on and two hundred more children who bore "a look of patient, hopeless suffering, terribly touching to see in such young children" were fed and clothed.

Adeline and Priscilla knew that their work that day was "only a drop in the ocean of misery"[48] and barely enough to postpone the inevitable unless they were able to establish a more regular distribution, and do so quickly.

They had already begun the most important task upon arriving in Knin, getting food to distribute to the starving masses. With the influx of the refuges, Indian corn, a major staple for the Bosnians under normal circumstances had almost doubled in price, and people were dying of starvation daily (a tenth of the fugitives having died between October and January). Adeline ordered £1000 worth of corn through the Belgian Consul in Rijeka (Fiume), enough to generously feed two thousand grown men for a month, and sent to Pakrac for Lazar Kovačević, a man they called Old Lazar, who had proven himself to be wise and trustworthy in their work in Slavonia, to oversee the distribution. In this one decision, the ladies did more than provide free food to the desperate refugees; they also forced the price of corn down to more reasonable levels. When the desperately needed food arrived in Knin on

January 16, the ladies immediately began taking it out to the surrounding towns.

Food, though, was not enough. They also ordered calico from Šibenik and Rijeka to make clothes and began distributing materials that had been sent from England for use against the cold mountain winters. They were making preparations to provide housing for those who still did not have a roof over their heads, but lumber in Dalmatia was scarce and expensive. If the refugees could stay warm and dry and well-fed, perhaps the outbreaks of smallpox, diphthoritis, and typhus which were decimating the camps could be impeded.

These were the pressing needs of the refugees and the ladies were taking immediate action. An article appeared in *The Times* on January 24—the majority of which is a letter from Adeline dated "Knin, January 9th"—was a testament to their endeavors. Gone were the amateur benefactresses who had taken two months to make any significant progress in Slavonia, and in their place were two experienced and confident humanitarians ordering and distributing resources, making much of the little they had and presenting a compelling case for why they should be entrusted with more.

In England, the Balkans were in the newspapers daily: reports from the uprisings in Bosnia and Bulgaria, graphic accounts of atrocities against civilians, transcripts from meetings of parliamentarians discussing the best solution to the "Eastern Question." The front page headlines brought an increased interest in the region and a renewed demand for Adeline and Georgina's book *Travels in the Slavonic Provinces of*

Turkey-in-Europe. At last giving in to her publisher's request for a revised edition, Adeline returned to England in March of 1877 to prepare the work for re-publication. Although it must have been difficult for the ladies to withdraw themselves from their ongoing work in Dalmatia, the distribution continued in the trusted hands of three resident Austrian gentlemen and Old Lazar, aided by Austrian officials and a woman named Countess Janković, who had started a school for girls in Daruvar before the war and in whose home the provisions were stored. This second edition also presented an opportunity to advance the fund and their labor for the refugees that could not be passed up. Adeline was now seen as an authority on Bosnia. In the preface to this second edition released April 1877, William Gladstone, former British Prime Minister and renowned statesman, wrote that, in his opinion, "no diplomatist, no consul, no traveller, among our countrymen, has made such valuable contribution to our means of knowledge in this important matter, as was made by Miss Mackenzie and Miss Irby, when they published, in 1867, their travels." He called their journey "one which would never have been undertaken except by ladies endowed with a courage and resolution as remarkable as their discernment and their benevolence." He also made reference to Adeline's current work as the source of her reliability, stating, "Miss Irby, after her long and self-sacrificing experience, speaks with a weight of dispassionate authority, to which neither I nor any correspondent of a public journal can pretend." This was high praise from an influential man, adding credibility and weight to Adeline's words, value that would hopefully result in more copies sold. The profit from the sales would go directly to the fund, and through the directresses, to feeding, clothing, and sheltering the exiled Bosnians.

When Adeline and Priscilla first arrived in Dalmatia in early January 1877 the refugee population was at a low point (10,000), a large number having moved north to the town of Gračac in a region then called the Upper Military Frontier and 10 percent having died of starvation and disease. The ladies returned, however, to a much different situation. The shaky peace that had held since November was broken from the outside when Russia declared war on Turkey in April of 1877. Fresh waves of Bosnians flooded across the border seeking safety, while the Austrian government struggled to face the increasing immigration problem. In late March, Austrian aid had been drastically decreased in hopes that the exiles would return to their land, but the renewed conflict ensured the continuation (and growth) of the refugee population. One-third of the Christian population of Bosnia was homeless.

In the small town of Plavno, thirteen miles to the north of Knin, a two and a half hour ride by cart, the ladies began an extensive work to provide adequate housing for the refugees. They purchased a piece of land near to the river and began constructing what became, over time, a small village of sheds. Over one hundred families were moved from the streets into these new homes where they were protected from the elements. Once the homes were established, they also opened a new school and orphanage right in the middle of the village. How the atmosphere must have changed: women busy making new clothes with material and thread they received;

children rushing to and from school, singing songs and re-viewing what they were learning; able-bodied men return-ing from the fields where they were tending the flax, maize, oats, and onions planted with donated seeds. The misery of life as a refugee continued, but the ladies' efforts were making it more bearable.

Arthur Evans, who visited this settlement, said that the Bosnians looked on the ladies with "a kind of veneration, and natives [came] from afar to see the two English queens—'Krajlice' as they called them."[49] The first village was such a success that the "two queens" decided to build another on the hillside above the town. Every fifteen days provisions were sent from Knin and distributed among these villages. Often Adeline would join the distribution, going from shed to shed, visiting with the families, checking in on the school, ensuring that the supplies were efficiently and adequately partitioned. Petar Mirković, who as a young man worked as secretary and assistant to Adeline and traveled with her many times to Plavno, wrote, perhaps with a bit of the exaggerated veneration mentioned by Mr. Evans:

> *For people that lived there, Miss Irby's visit would have been the happiest day in their lives. It was a day of comfort, because she came, a noble soul, who does not ask: Who are you? What are you? but: Where does it hurt and what do you need? She was the sunshine that shines much brighter than any spring sun.*
>
> *She came into the sheds, hands full, and gave to everyone, nurtured the sick without asking if the*

disease was transferable. She gave them medicine and other necessities. Those who were really sick she sent to a hospital immediately. She gave robes, money, bread, sugar, tea and cocoa. Even though I witnessed all of this, my weak pen cannot explain or describe the noble sacrifice, the mercy and kindness to the poor and miserable people. If I peeked into the history of mankind, I couldn't find an example anywhere to which I could compare those deeds of the Noble Adeline Irby.[50]

For one group of families living in the villages, Adeline and Priscilla had done more than simply make their lives easier; they had saved them. In the winter of 1877 a large relief caravan headed from Knin across the mountains and into northwestern Bosnia. Despite the warnings that the wintery roads were too difficult, Adeline chose to go along. At Stožišta, past Strmica and in the mountains, a snowstorm caught the party by surprise. The wind whipped the snow up into the travelers' eyes, decreasing visibility to a few feet, frightening the horses and sending some of their riders into the powder. Progress was slow. Petar, who was a part of the expedition, noted that instead of showing fear, Adeline seemed to be laughing. Perhaps the adventure reminded her of earlier days with Georgina or the thrill she used to experience roaming about the region, before the refugee crisis demanded her complete focus. For whatever reason, Adeline laughed as they pressed on, heads down against the wind, barely escaping with their lives. At last they arrived at Peći, a village at the base of the Dinara Mountain.

That night, Adeline shared a 500-square-foot shed with a refugee family. In the middle of the room, which represented the whole of the shack, was a fireplace; and in one corner was all that the family possessed, one cow. She slept on a bed of pine leaves and branches lifted off the floor by four stones onto which water constantly dripped from above, the seeping of melted snow through the pine branch roof. The smoke in the room was so great that Adeline wondered how the family did not go blind from constant exposure. The next morning, she surprised the family by paying for the use of their bed an amount that would have afforded her a night in the most comfortable hotel in Vienna.

The next morning they set out early for Resanovci and then turned west into the mountains and towards their destination: the caves of Dinara. The horses, packed down with food, clothing and supplies, struggled to keep their footing as they ascended the steep, narrow path. Each step forward represented progress, but also made progressing more difficult, bringing higher altitudes, colder air, deeper snow. All the while, the cliff dropped off abruptly just past the edge of the ribbon-thin passageway.

Reaching the first cave, Adeline entered. She slowly made her way down the steep entrance, which eventually opened up into a large chamber, the majority of which was blanketed in darkness. She put her hand on the wall to let her eyes adjust. It was wet. The sound of dripping water filled the dark, echoing up from an underground lake somewhere deep in the cavern, trickling off dripstone onto the damp floor. There was a small bonfire in the corner of the room. Around it there appeared to float thirteen sets of eyes, the owners of which were too blackened with soot and dirt to be visible.

Adeline laid a small blanket on the floor with some bread on it.

She waited.

At last a cry broke the drone of the water's music: "Mom, I'm hungry! I'm hungry!"

Then, from around the fire, came seven walking skeletons, hardly covered by the torn rags that once were their clothes, and six smaller figures, bare feet splashing on the watery floor. They were seven widows and their children. Looking at them was like facing death, a scene impossible to forget. Almost fifty years later Petar wrote: "Those who have never seen something like this do not know what human suffering is. Do not know how black and miserable life is! Do not know true pain or how to pray to God for safety from miseries like that."[51]

Adeline began to cry.

The tears running down her cheeks joined the puddles at her feet. But Adeline was not mourning. She was crying for joy. In that moment she knew, without doubt, that she had found a purpose. Not only had she found it, she was fulfilling it. She was right where she was supposed to be, doing exactly what God wanted her to do. Perhaps the whirlwind of the past twenty years rushed through her mind—the Carpathians, the bungling *Beamter*, travels in the Balkans, the school in Sarajevo. How did she end up here? Perhaps she thought back on the times she almost gave up, preferring to stay in London and enjoy the life of a noble or remain at Lea Hurst with Florence. What if she had never come? What would have become of those here?

Perhaps she understood, again, the Christian hymn she had taught the children in the schools:

Abide with me; fast falls the eventide;
The darkness deepens; Lord with me abide.

When other helpers fail and comforts flee,
Help of the helpless, O abide with me.

I fear no foe, with Thee at hand to bless;
Ills have no weight, and tears no bitterness.
Where is death's sting? Where, grave, thy victory?
I triumph still, if Thou abide with me.[52]

God was with her. God had led her here into the darkness, face to face with death. God was defeating death before her very eyes. And he was using her to do it. Adeline cried with joy.

The widows and children were moved to new homes down in the valley and given everything they needed to live. By that summer, many more families had been rescued from the Dinarite grottoes, released from their graves and given a second chance at life.

KOMŠIJA JE NAJBLIŽI

"Love the Lord your God with all your heart and with all your soul and with all your mind and with all your strength." The second is this: "Love your neighbor as yourself." There is no commandment greater than these.
—The Bible, Mark 12:30-31[53]

A T NOON ON a Wednesday I stepped through the street level door of a purple, Austrian-style, corner building in the heart of Sarajevo. The building had been constructed in 1911 to house the offices of the educational and cultural society Prosvjeta. I entered into a medium-sized reading room with long tables encircled by chairs and a bookshelf against the wall. An older woman sitting at the far table with papers spread out in front of her welcomed me with a smile and directed me to a seat across from her. As the president of the Prosvjeta board of directors, she was the one I came to speak with. I had heard that her organization tries to keep the memory of Miss Irby alive.

Prosvjeta, according to their promotional brochure, was founded in 1902 to advance the cause of education among the underprivileged villagers of Bosnia, a purpose they continue to carry out today, giving university and high school scholarships to students. According to their brochure they are non-governmental, non-religious, and non-political; they seek to spread the idea of democracy and unity among citizens of all nationalities. After talking for a few minutes about some of the organization's recent activities—especially the ecumenical Christmas concert that was supported by many of the other cultural societies—the conversation turned towards Miss Irby.

"I know that here at Prosvjeta there is a Miss Irby Women's Club. Why do you think it is important," I asked, "to remember Miss Irby and her life?"

"Miss Irby is a great woman in the history of Bosnia and Herzegovina. She is someone who left her country and her very rich family to help the Bosnian people. With her own money she established some of the first schools for young girls who couldn't afford to pay for their schooling."

"Yes," I agreed, "Miss Irby made many sacrifices to help the Bosnian people. What about today, though? What is the message of her life? What do Miss Irby's actions say to young people in Bosnia today?"

"It is simple: Do good, fight against evil, fight against wars."

As she said the last part, her expression changed a bit and the tenor of her voice lowered.

"Of course, Sarajevo just passed through a terrible chaos. I was here the whole time. As a Serb. That was why we wanted to hold that Christmas Concert. We wanted to show that there are still people from the Orthodox faith in Sarajevo. That we are citizens of this city who respect others. We are . . ." she paused as if searching for the right phrase, "We are nobody's Serbs. We love this city and we belong to this city. We are Sarajevans."

The director of the board was born in Baščaršija quite near to the Sebilj, the Turkish fountain at the heart of the old town. Her family later moved to Novo Sarajevo where she and her husband remained throughout the duration of the '90s. Her family has always been connected to the artistic and cultural life of the city: her husband, who died only three years before, was an Opera singer; her son and his wife are members of the Opera choir; she finished the secondary school of music. When the war started, they couldn't bring themselves to leave, although that would have been the easier choice.

"What did your neighbors think about the fact that you stayed?" I asked, curious what it must have been like to be a Serb in the city while there were Serbs surrounding the city.

"There was no difference. Neighbors are the most important. There is family; then there are your neighbors. *Komšija je najbliži*. This is the message of Miss Irby: love others and appreciate the differences between us."

There is a story I have known since the earliest time I can remember; one that I heard, like many kids around the world, on a Sunday morning or from my parents at bedtime, a story from the Bible which was also read to the children in Adeline's school. The story of the Good Samaritan.

An educated religious man came to Jesus in order to test him and see firsthand if his teaching was the truth. This

---

*   literally, A neighbour is the closest.

religious scholar asked Jesus, "What do I need to do to get eternal life?" The crowd all turned to Jesus, eager to hear his answer, but Jesus, as he often did, turned the attention back on his questioner, "What do you think? How do you interpret God's Law?" Heads turned back in the direction of the scholar who now found himself on the defensive.

"Love the Lord your God with all your heart, mind, soul, and strength; and love your neighbor as you love yourself," he replied, quoting the verses from the Torah that he had known since childhood. "Good answer!" Jesus said encouragingly. Then, after a pause, "Do this and you will live."

The scholar stood there, probably a little disappointed with the way this conversation had gone, thinking about what Jesus had said. He was a detailed man, trained in the finer points of the Law, and this standard that Jesus had set was far too ambiguous and vast. How could he know when he had loved God and others enough? Was he supposed to love everyone the same? Was he even supposed to love the evil Romans who were occupying his country by the strength of their swords? Or the irreligious and immoral Samaritans living to the north? Searching for a loophole, he asked another question: "Who is my neighbor?"

It was then that Jesus told a story:

"There was once a man traveling from Jerusalem to Jericho. On the way he was attacked by robbers. They took his clothes, beat him up, and went off leaving him half-dead. Luckily, a priest was on his way down the same road, but when he saw him he angled across to the other side. Then a religious man showed up; he also avoided the injured man.

"A Samaritan traveling the road came on him. When he saw the man's condition, his heart went out to him. He gave him first aid, disinfecting and bandaging his wounds. Then he lifted him onto his donkey, led him to an inn, and made him comfortable. In the morning he took out two silver coins and gave them to the innkeeper, saying, 'Take good care of him. If it costs any more, put it on my bill—I'll pay you on my way back.'"

The crowd was silent as Jesus finished the story, watching to see what he would do next. Jesus turned to the religious scholar and asked, "Which one of these three proved to be a neighbor to the man who was beaten by the robbers?"

"The one who showed mercy," was the scholar's response.

"You go and do the same."

The conversation was over. Jesus had made his point and the scholar, who had come to test Jesus, had learned his lesson. He had been asking the wrong question. The right question was not "Who is my neighbor?" The better question—the one which the scholar did not want to ask—was more personal. This question was like a high wattage light bulb shining upon his heart, exposing not only his actions but also the true condition of his soul. "What kind of neighbor am I?"

A visitor to one of Adeline's refugee schools in Slavonia listened in as the professor quizzed the students. After displaying a proficiency in spelling, reading, writing, and simple arithmetic, the subject turned to the Bible. One child was asked to recite the parable of the Good Samaritan, which he did, with a few slight changes: instead of robbers, the man on the road was attacked by *Hajduks* and the Levite was replaced by a *Paroh*, a local church official. When the student finished his adapted tale, another boy was asked by the teacher to explain the meaning of the 'neighbor' in the story.

"Suppose today, on your way home, you saw someone in need by the road. Would you help him even if he was not like you, a Serb, but instead a Hungarian, or a Jew, or a Turk?"

The youth knew the correct answer and was prepared to give it, that is, until the professor's last word. He was exiled because of the Turkish troops that had driven his family from their land. Perhaps his father or uncle or cousin were at that moment fighting against the sultan's forces or had already been killed by them. "Not a Turk!" the youth answered decisively.

Then, from the back of the room, came the milder voice of another student: "Yes, I would help him, even if he was a Turk. That is what neighbors are supposed to do."[54]

Adeline was a good neighbor. She found not just one man, but a whole nation lying wounded by the road. With her own resources she bandaged, fed and cared for those in need. Reverend Shaffer, the pastor of the Evangelical Church in Sarajevo during Adeline's lifetime, described her saying, "She did not ask if the orphans spoke English or were they evangelicals by faith, but wherever she had seen misery she helped. Who doesn't know the story of the Good Samaritan? Here we have a Samaritan like the heart of our Lord Jesus Christ. And once she had felt the happiness of knowing what it means to be able to help the Lord, there was no other way for her. She understood the words of God, completely and utterly: What you've done to one of my little brothers, you've done to me as well."

REFUGEE WORK OPPOSED

1877-1878

*[Miss Irby and Miss Johnston] have labored here from some
months with more than woman's strength, but with their whole
soul in the work and God's blessing on them. Here both the
people and press say: "If it had not been for the heroic efforts
of those English ladies, thousands and thousands more lives
would have been sacrificed."*
—June27, 1877, *Daily News*[55]

*Never were those pernicious questions asked: Who are you?
Why are you here? What is your faith? Where have you come
from? Only one question was asked:
What do you need? And it was given.*
—Dorothy Anderson, *Miss Irby and her Friends*[56]

ADELINE AND PRISCILLA'S work continued to grow and expand throughout 1877. The schools—which increased from 1,800 students in April to over 2,000 in July—numbered 22 by the end of the year with 23 schoolmasters and one schoolmistress. Inside each schoolhouse was a blackboard, a few globes to teach geography, a small library of books—some translated from English, others containing national history and songs, and modern translations of the New Testament—and on the walls hung color pictures of nature, history, and biblical events. The teachers were passionate and motivated and the eager students were quick to learn.

The ladies knew that they were not simply rescuing these children from the suffering of refugee life; they were making an investment in the future of Bosnia. Perhaps one day, they thought, when the war ended, these children, knowing how to read and write, and these teachers, trained in pedagogy, would return to their own land and rebuild their society. Arthur Evans agreed. One chapter of his book, *The Illyrian Chronicles*, is entitled, "The Hope of Bosnia: Miss Irby and Miss Johnston's Children." He was struck by the contrast between life inside of the school and life outside of it. He was amazed by the "civilization and refinement" he saw in the schoolmasters and the brightness of the students. He noted that the children six-years-old and up were learning to read and write in only three months, and that education was having an effect even outside of the school walls.

Evans told of one boy who, after learning the basics at school, was apprenticed out to a local businessman as a swineherd. The hours he spent in the woods with the pigs prevented him from attending the school further, but he took with him a book of songs and a New Testament as well as some paper to continue working on his writing. Arthur said of the boy, "education seems to have given a greater capacity for the business of life; so much so that the lad's master declared the other day that 'there never was such a good swineherd.'" The schools, which gave hope for Bosnia's future, were drastically changing the present culture for these children. There was no comparison between the picture inside the schoolhouse and outside of it. Again, Arthur Evans provides the best description:

> There is a vision of girls who are hags before they are women; of human pigmies distorted by exposure and disease, and wasted away by hunger, staring the blank, stupid stare of idiocy—a vision of the supreme corruption of the most beautiful; but, then, a vision of row on row of pretty, childish forms, neatly ranged on their small school benches, neither starved nor naked; of cheerful, fresh expressions—lashes quivering with the breath of a newly-awakened intelligence, as I have seen the tender sprays of a Bosnian forest stirred by the April breeze; and a starlight of quick eyes twinkling forth from those half-dreamy child faces, like morning stars of a brighter life.[57]

Yet, this second vision was under imminent threat. The Bosnian and Herzegovinian Fugitives and Orphan Relief Fund was running desperately low, new refugees were crossing the border daily, and the menacing hand of politics was soon to disrupt everything.

*   *   *

The success of Adeline and Priscilla's organization demanded a balancing act of complex and competing needs. They
had wisely delegated the work of feeding, clothing and educating the children to trusted officials and local helpers, but,
Adeline discovered, this 'native machinery' would slow and
even come to a stop were she not constantly applying fire to
the engine. A fire's heat is only felt at close range. What about
the other necessary fuel: money? The ladies required £300 (today's equivalent of $25,000) each month simply to maintain
the schools and care for the 72 orphans they were housing.
Add to that the cost of food (£7,000 from January to August
1877 just for Indian corn), cloth, and lumber for the remaining refugee population. Though they were able to publish letters and advertisements for the fund in the major papers back
in Britain, there was no substitute for their presence. They
were pulled in two directions: remaining in Dalmatia would
result in their resources drying up, but returning to England
could mean the misapplication of those resources. In the end,
they had to entrust the work to others so that their efforts
could be given a chance to continue.

Although these trips back to England were not for the purpose of vacationing—their days were filled with writing reports, reconciling accounts, publishing pamphlets, and attending events—the time with friends and family away from
the constant needs of the refugees was restorative. Every day
on the frontier, Adeline and Priscilla were placing their own
health at risk. Dalmatia's bone-chilling winter *Bura* and stifling summer heat; the air in the storehouse, thick with dust,
and in the homes of refugees, damp and infused with disease;

the long hours of labor and sleepless nights; these all left an impression on their well-being. Back in Britain, Adeline often visited Lea Hurst, the home of Florence Nightingale. There she spent time with Florence and her mother, regaining her strength, and writing as she did the summer of 1877. Perhaps it gave her extra strength to know that while she was enjoying the cool, clean air of the English countryside, Professor Josić was in Pakrac with all of the schoolteachers from Slavonia and Dalmatia for a two month training course. The instructors stayed together in the nicest hotel in town with all of their expenses paid for by Adeline and the money she was in the process of collecting.

When Adeline and Priscilla left England for the frontier on October 17, the fund was replenished—£7,000 were received in two months and a representative was found to collect donations in the United States. Filled with renewed strength, the ladies' first published letter that fall included a glowing report of the institutions they had inspected. In one school, they arrived unannounced to find two Bosnian teachers and one hundred twenty students diligently at work. After examining the students they found that "no time had been wasted." The schools, which to them were the most important aspect of their work, were not only surviving, but growing and thriving.

The women were overjoyed. But during the winter of 1878, all of that changed. All but five schools were closed.

Adeline and Priscilla faced resistance throughout their time in Slavonia and Dalmatia. The first couple months the opposition came from the refugees themselves, who could not trust that the two foreign English ladies were not hiding some sinister motive. Then, as they gained the confidence of the fugitives, various government sources began applying pressure. One such example was a relief expedition sent by the ladies from Dalmatia to the region across the mountain range that separated Austrian controlled Dalmatia from Hungarian administered Croatia. The wagons, which were piled high with clothes and coverings for the refugees, were stopped at the snowy ridge of Mount Velebit by Hungarian custom agents. It was common practice at the time for nations to forgo the application of customs dues for humanitarian supplies in times of distress, which the Austrian officials upheld. But it was not so in Hungarian territory. The customs officials began to rip open the bags; prod and poke them with sharp medal rods; cast shirts, blankets, and clothes onto the roadside; upend, unwrap, and empty every container. Arthur Evans, who was with the expedition, noted that if another traveler would have happened upon the scene, he would have assumed that the carts were being attacked by a gang of robbers.[58] After a laborious process of calculation, the officials demanded a tax that was so high and so impossible to pay, that seven hundred of the warmest, heaviest coats had to be left behind, while what remained proceeded on to the shivering women and children who had hidden themselves among the snow-covered mountains along the border.

As a rule, the Austrian government, overwhelmed by the presence of 150,000 refugees on their soil, was more supportive of Adeline and Priscilla's work. In Knin, a number of Austrian gendarmes assisted the ladies with distribution of supplies and identifying needy families fleeing across the border from Hercegovina. As the war evolved and Russia's involvement and success against Turkish forces foreshadowed a greater Austrian presence in the region, the relationship between the Austrian government and the Bosnian refugees would change. Adeline had already waded through a mire of governmental bureaucracy in the process of opening her schools, usually overcoming it through the force of her will, the testimony of her powerful connections, and her British passport. But in February 1878, a new opposition began.

The new governor of the Croatian Military Frontier, General Filipović, forbid Professor Josić and his assistants from any further involvement in the schools, accusing them of behavior "dangerous to public order and tranquility." The problem with this allegation was that it was untrue, as was confirmed by the inspectors who came to examine the schools and could find no treasonable activities. The professor was, as Adeline had come to know, a hard-working and honest man of the highest character. When no charges could be substantiated against him, he was removed by way of a technical flaw in his diploma.

Perhaps Adeline and Priscilla could have dealt with the professor's absence were it not for the fact that the governor, not wanting to lose the benefit of English charity among the refugees, appointed his own supervisor for the schools. The man chosen was wholly unfit for the position and detested by the teachers he would be required to manage. Adeline felt that she was left with only one choice. She couldn't send money to be managed by someone she did not know and did not trust—that same money could go to feed, clothe, and house the refugees in areas where trusted associates were working. Therefore, the schools were closed.

* * *

Had the professor been accused of being a Slav or a Serb, or the schools accused of teaching Serbian literature and history, then the claim would have been affirmed. The majority of refugees with which Adeline worked were Bosnian Serbs. This, of course, was due to the fact that the majority of refugees from Bosnia were Serbian farmers. She wrote to a friend: "we have helped Pravoslavs [Orthodox] (because those who were in need of help happened to be Pravoslavs)."[59] Adeline, who had experienced the de-nationalization of Slavs in other areas of the world, was adamant that the children in her schools would understand their own history and literature and appreciate their own religious heritage.

While Adeline worked primarily with the Orthodox from Bosnia and Herzegovina, she did not do so exclusively. Some of the orphans in her care were Catholic, and she worked hard to find them good homes within Catholic families. On 24 October 1877 an appeal was made in the leading newspaper of Ireland "at the instance of two Protestant ladies, Miss Irby and Miss Johnston" for funds to be given to support the work of the Irish Sisters of Charity and "to save the poor orphans of Catholic parents."[60] The article goes on to affirm the work of the Sisters, who were laboring "at much peril to their lives." The irony of this situation cannot be overstated: two Protestant English women appealing to Catholics in Ireland, where the citizens were divided by religion (Protestant versus Catholic), in order to raise funds for Catholic Humanitarian work in the Balkans, where the citizens were divided by religion (Catholic versus Orthodox versus Muslim). Her involvement was determined by need rather than religion.

Once, while overseeing the distribution of provisions in Strmica, a large group of Muslims arrived seeking help, having traveled over forty miles on foot, through the snow and over the Dinarite, from Orašac. It was rare for Muslims to come to Strmica. When word reached Adeline of their presence in the town, one of the workers who was near her replied:

"I wouldn't give them anything! They have their house and lands." Then, perhaps thinking about his own home in Bosnia that stood vacant and his fields that remained unplowed and unsown, he continued, "they don't have needs like we do."

Adeline turned to him. "Let me ask you a question," she said, smiling as she spoke. "Can a Muslim be poor? Can a Muslim be hungry?"

"Yes," the man replied, not lifting his eyes to meet hers, "he can."

"Then surely those people must be poor and hungry since they came here." Then with a softer voice, one that caused the young man to look up, she said, "Bring them in so that we can read their faces. It is face to face that one can really know a man, his character and his motives."

The families were brought inside, half of them shuffling in the remains of what were once shoes, the other half barefoot, clutching about them their scraps of clothes, almost naked against the cold. Their faces were legible: desperate, bone-tired, despondent, nearly lifeless. They had already buried one of their number on the way, just six miles from the town. There would be no hope of finding his body on the way back since it was carried away in the blizzard; his family would be without a father or the closure of a proper burial.

"Enough," Adeline said quietly. And then to the young worker beside her, "I have heard enough. Their faces say:

We are hungry, barefoot, naked! Our children cry for help."

The room was silent. Adeline, again smiling as she spoke, said to the group, "You will have everything you need."

When the families left Strmica they had food, clothes, money, tools, and other necessary supplies. Adeline also sent money and clothes for the family of the man who died on the way, to comfort the children grieving the loss of their father.

As greatly as this incident affected these Muslim families, perhaps the more enduring effect was on those in Strmica who witnessed it. Such was the impact on one young man, Petar, that 45 years later, in his book about Miss Irby, he would recount the event in detail.

Petar also wrote about another incident. While Adeline and Priscilla were in Knin, refugees would come to them every day asking for help; no one was sent away without receiving some kind of assistance, whether food or money or something else. They did not, however, always get what they asked for.

One day, a peasant from a small town in Bosnia, came to the school in Knin in search of help.

"I need to speak with the Noble," he petitioned Petar, who was, at the time, working as Adeline's secretary.

Petar went into the house. "Noble, there is a visitor here from Bosnia seeking help."

"Send him in."

When the poor man entered, Adeline asked, "What is it that you want?"

"Please, ma'am, give me a rifle," he said, shifting his weight back and forth, a little unsure of how to behave in the presence of "The Noble."

"Why do you need a rifle?"

"I would like to join the uprising," he replied, uncomfortably, "but I don't have a rifle."

Adeline stood up and took a step towards the man. "Do you know how to read?"

"I do."

"Excuse me one moment," Adeline said, walking into an adjacent room. After a few moments she returned with a Bible in her hand. "Take this book," she offered with a smile, "there are all kinds of weapons in it. There are rifles, cannons, knives and swords. You can defeat all of your enemies easily with this book without shedding a single drop of blood. It will give your life comfort and bring you victory and happiness."

The peasant took the book from her and stood silently, holding it in his hand.

"How many children do you have?" Adeline inquired.

"Five."

"How old are they?"

The man listed their names and ages, but seemed a little bit disappointed, as if trying to figure out how a book would help him defeat his enemies.

"Well," Adeline said, "you came looking for a rifle. Do you want to see my deadliest weapons? I have them downstairs in the yard."

Adeline motioned the way and the man descended the stairs to find a garden full of orphan children, all cleanly dressed, running about and playing together. After a short while, Adeline joined the man, who was now flipping through the Bible with interest, as if he was really looking for a weapon inside. She grinned.

"These are my brightest and most deadly weapons," she said kindly to the man, motioning to the children. She handed him a large bag of clothes and some money saying, "Take this to your children, but look after the weapon well and live by it. It will protect you in life and make you invincible to your enemies."

That afternoon, as the man returned home, the war became one person smaller and five children received their father as if back from the dead.

The new governor of the Croatian frontier viewed Adeline as he would any other insurgent, stirring up ancient hatreds detrimental to his government's authority. He viewed her children, whom Arthur Evans called "the hope of Bosnia", as a threat to the state. But these students—Adeline's most deadly weapons—were aimed only against ignorance, poverty and hatred. With great care she armed them with love for their enemies and forgiveness for those who wronged them.

When the schools across Slavonia were closed, three remained open in and around Pakrac (an area distinct from the Military Frontier). The mayor of the town, a Croatian and a Roman Catholic, pleaded with Adeline to keep the schools open, even offering to supervise them personally. Knowing him to be a "humane and liberal man" she agreed, continuing to support the schools financially until the end of the uprising.

18

PROTEST AND REFORM

To sin by silence, when they should protest, makes cowards of men.
—Ella Wheeler Wilcox, author and poet[61]

"WHAT ARE YOU protesting?" a friend asked me.
I gave him a confused look from across the table. "What do you mean?"

"Well, you said that you are a Protestant. So, what are you protesting?"

I wasn't sure how to answer. I simply stared back at him for an uncomfortable length of time and then said something to cover the silence. Whatever I said, I don't remember. But I remember his question.

Up until then I had never spent enough time thinking about the word "Protestant" to realize that it is rooted in the word "protest". I did not feel like I was protesting against anything. As I thought about it more, it began to make sense. It also helped me make sense of Adeline. I realized that I could not understand her apart from her Protestant Christian faith.

★   ★   ★

I grew up in a Protestant Christian home. We were very involved in our church, but that could be expected since my Dad was the minister. He was not the normal clergy type, though. For one, he didn't like for people to call him "reverend" or "pastor". Sometimes, when people would try to call him Reverend Irby he would respond, "What makes me more deserving of reverence that anybody else? If you want to revere someone, revere God." He was usually straightforward like that. He felt more comfortable spending time with people outside of the church than he did with other ministers. Perhaps that had to do with his past.

My father was a convinced atheist until he was 24. He not only rebelled against the idea of God, but also any other authority figure who tried to exert himself over his life. He lived his life like a protest against the status quo. For him that meant cruising the highways in his purple convertible with yellow bucket seats, picking up as many girls as he could in the neighboring towns, and, in general, maximizing his fun while keeping his responsibility to a minimum. This worked until he found a girl who was resistant to his advances. She did accept his offer for a date, but on one condition: their date would be on Sunday morning at church. He went. That first date—the church service, the conversation over lunch afterwards—sent him on a philosophical journey in which he explored all the various religions he had earlier rejected. In the end, he chose Christianity. A year later, he and the girl married. A year after that, he enrolled at a local seminary to become a minister.

In seminary he did not lose his rebelliousness. It simply changed. He began to voraciously read the Bible, to apply the truth he found there to all areas of his life, and to faithfully live as a believer in God. There was a reformation in his life. He was still rebellious, though. He rebelled against any authority that attempted to speak for God or place itself more significant than the Bible. In Protestantism, his rebellion found a higher purpose: he became a protestor *for* God instead of *against* him.

That was the world I grew up in.

In many ways he reminds me of Adeline: a little hard-headed, resistant to the status quo, accepting no authority other than God. He also reminds me of the guy who started the whole protest from which Protestants arose, Martin Luther.

Martin, who was born in Germany in 1483, had his life mapped out for him. He planned to become a lawyer—a noble profession for a miner's son—and provide for himself and his family. But one day he was caught in a thunderstorm so fierce that he was knocked to the ground by a bolt of lightning. Fearing for his life, he called out to one of the Catholic saints, "St. Anne, save me! And I'll become a monk." He survived the storm and, much to his parent's disappointment, kept his promise. This one event not only changed the course of Martin's life, it precipitated a revolution in Europe that still reverberates.

On October 31, 1517, 12 years after surviving the thunderstorm, Martin Luther nailed a list of 95 complaints against the Catholic Church to the wooden door of the Castle Church in Wittenberg, the town where he was a monk and seminary professor. He hoped that his "95 Theses" would lead to reform within his church, the Church of Rome, which had been in a state of decline and division for two centuries. In the end, his protest started a storm that even he could not control. It was this "Reformation" that led to the branch of Christianity that came to be called Protestantism.

"What is Protestantism all about?" I solicited, opening the discussion.

I was sitting in an office at the University of Sarajevo with a history professor and two of her students. A few months before, the students had met a friend of mine while searching for a Protestant to interview for a project in their European history class. The teacher explained that many of her history students have a hard time understanding Protestant Christianity, since most of them come from a Muslim background. We were meeting so that I could hear what the students were learning about Protestantism and gain an outside perspective on Adeline's faith.

"Reading and understanding the Bible is central to what Protestants believe," the professor began. "Martin Luther, and the other Reformers of his time, understood the need to translate the Bible into the everyday language of the people so that they could understand it. Luther translated the Bible into German and people suddenly realized that they could read it themselves. At that time, thanks to Gutenberg and his printing press," she continued, "it was cheaper to print books. Literature was more accessible and it was possible to learn."

"But one of the problems in that time," interjected Mustafa, a third year history major who sat cross-legged, looking through dark-rimmed glasses, "is that people couldn't read. There was a lot of illiteracy."

"Yes," the professor agreed, "the early Protestants realized that they had to fight against illiteracy. Education was very important to them."

"That makes sense," I added. "One of the mottoes of the Reformation that I learned in church was *sola scriptura*, which is Latin for 'the scriptures alone'. They believed that the Bible was the highest authority for understanding the truth about God and the world. Not even the Church or the Pope could be above the Bible. If the Bible is the highest authority then people need to be able to read so that they can have access to it."

"You can see this with Luther," Mustafa contributed. "He read the Bible and found all of these things in it that were contrary to what he was seeing in the Church around him."

"The sale of indulgences was one of those things," the professor added. "In fact, it was the main thing that inspired Luther to write his 95 theses. Indulgences were a way for people to 'buy' forgiveness from the Church. It did not matter if you were sorry for what you did or if you were willing to change. If you had money, you could be forgiven. You could even buy indulgences for people who were already dead so that their punishment in the afterlife would be shorter. The most famous salesman of indulgences was a man named Teztel who said, 'As soon as a coin in the coffer rings, a soul from purgatory springs.' Our students can easily understand why this was wrong."

The two students nodded their heads, affirming her statement.

"The indulgences made Luther angry," I responded. "Through studying the Bible, Luther came to believe that

God's forgiveness could not be bought or earned. It was given to those who believed, through the undeserved goodness of God. The two Reformation phrases—*sola gratia*, 'by grace alone,' and *sola fide*, 'by faith alone'—summarized that idea. Luther's realization came while reading a section of the Bible written by Paul that says, 'The righteousness of God is revealed from faith to faith, as it is written, "The righteous shall live by faith".'[62] Luther, who almost became a lawyer, understood what it meant for someone to be *righteous* or *just*. It meant that they were not guilty, as in a court of law. Here he saw the Bible saying that people are made 'just' not through their good works or through an institution, but simply through faith in God. That, to Luther, was grace."

The other student, Naida, also a third year history major, jumped in, "They understood that they had a direct connection with God; they did not need someone in between them. God does not go through the Pope or through a king to them, there is a direct connection between them. And that is a revolutionary thing in religion!"

"It was decentralization," I agreed. "The control and the power were transferred into the hands of the people. They could read the Bible and understand it. They could respond to what it said with faith. They could go directly to God for forgiveness."

I was impressed with how well the students understood these complex religious ideas. I had grown up with them my whole life; they had one class on them.

"There was also a change in the idea of the Church," the professor added. "For Protestants, the church is not only a building that you can see, but a spiritual community of all believers. This was new in the 16th century. This spiritual community—one you can experience but cannot see—was something radical."

"Right," I said. "It has the potential to take the emphasis off of labels and put it on the individual. Belonging to a certain church does not make someone a member of that spiritual community. What really matters is what that person believes and how they respond to God. Even having the label 'priest' does not guarantee that someone is a part of the spiritual community. Labels are not as important. A church member is just as important as a church leader; someone with a secular job is just as important as someone with a religious job."

"That is why Protestants were much more involved in business," said the professor. "It is the Protestant work ethic: work hard, live humbly, save your money, have a business. Through this they became very influential in society and, eventually, economics and politics."

"Luther started a fire that grew so big not even he could control it," I responded. "Once you take power from a few and put it in the hands of the people, no one can control the outcome."

"That is why I try to teach my students that the Reformation and Protestantism are so important to understanding European history," the professor concluded.

And, I thought as I said goodbye to the group and left the office, why it is so important to understanding Adeline.

Martin Luther, Adeline, my dad. They were all protesters. They protested against any authority above the Bible. They protested against any way to God except through faith. They protested against the idea that a church building made up the Church. They protested against the religious establishment. They were *Protest*ants.

I guess that makes me a protester too.

I remember one afternoon, when I was fifteen years old, walking into my dad's office at the church to talk with him. His personal library lined the room—8,000 books in all—and he sat behind a large oak desk writing in his unintelligible script. I had come to inform him that we were no longer in agreement. I was logging my dissent. I was nailing my theses to his office door. He listened patiently to my argument: how I felt his perspective was incomplete, how my perspective answered the questions his left exposed, how my perspective was the correct one. I realize now that he must have sat through hundreds of speeches like this during his time in ministry, but at the moment, I was sure I was the first to disagree with him.

I am not sure how I expected him to respond—would he scold me like a disobedient child?—or rebuke me for questioning his authority?—or correct my errant theology? I was surprised by the result. He smiled and looked up at me (I had remained standing during my discourse) and asked me a few clarifying questions. How did I answer *this* question? What did I think about *that* verse in the Bible? I gave a few impromptu answers (I had not thought about the question or the verse). He told me that he was glad I had thought it all out for myself and then went back to work.

Looking back on this event, I see that he was teaching me a Protestant perspective. He was far more concerned that I learn to think for myself than that I agree with him on every point of doctrine. Had he told me what to believe, he would have been placing himself in a position above the Bible, the book he had taught me to trust and respect. Perhaps he was proud that I was willing to stand up to him for something I believed was true. Perhaps he was proud I had learned how to protest.

After our conversation, I kept studying the issue. I re-read the verses from the Bible, re-examined my perspective, and questioned my conclusion. Within a year, I found that I no longer disagreed with my dad. My conclusion, though, was not based on his authority, but the authority of the Bible. Martin Luther would have been proud.

It is interesting how words, like Protestant, can lose their meaning over time. They lose their significance and power. They become ash instead of flame. This is especially true in the world of religion where labels and names get assigned to power and authority. There is no power in a label or a name. People can lose the meaning so easily. Adeline's faith, though, did not easily lose its power. It drove her to action. Martin Luther once said, "Good works do not make a man good, but a good man does good works." As I considered my conversation with the professor and the students, I believed that Adeline wholeheartedly agreed with that statement.

RETURN TO BOSNIA

1878-1879

Such help, though only a drop in the bucket of misery before us, is still grateful to these poor sufferers as a proof that they are not forgotten.

—Adeline Paulina Irby, on their refugee efforts[63]

O N NOVEMBER 14, 1878, the sun rose on 300 refugees huddled together at the entrance to Pakrac loading their only possessions into the eight awaiting carts. The women and children, who made up the majority of the rabble, were dressed cleanly in their freshly washed, white calico shirts and woolen aprons, and their heads covered with red-bordered white handkerchiefs; the men, mostly aged, shuffled about, children darting in and out between their unsteady legs. Among them, distributing blankets and bread, clothing and shoes were Adeline and Priscilla. The return to Bosnia had begun.

Only a month earlier, 82,000 Austrian troops under the

leadership of General Filipović completed the occupation of Bosnia and Herzegovina. Now, eager to reverse the exodus of refugees and free the Austrian-controlled lands from the burden of their care, General Filipović had ordered the repatriation of all Bosnians and Herzegovins.

As this first detachment prepared to leave for home, a deep foreboding rested on the crowd. *Are we really to be sent back at the beginning of winter?* They understood the strain that the cold and wet three to four day journey would place on the delicate health of the elderly and sick. They also knew what awaited them once they arrived "home"; their houses would be piles of ash and rubble, and their fields would be overgrown with weeds and brush from three years of neglect. They pleaded with the Government to allow them to stay in Pakrac until spring, when they would gladly return to work the soil of their native land and could survive housed in simple wooden barracks or holes dug in the ground and covered with boughs. But in the depth of winter, those holes dug into the wet earth would become the graves of many. Their request had been denied.

The *podžupan* (municipal head) of Pakrac—the same man who was overseeing the remaining Slavonian schools—urgently requested help from Adeline and Priscilla and resources from their fund. When the ladies arrived, they immediately bought up all of the warm woolen blankets and leather shoes that the town could afford to sell and began delivering them to the neediest. As they looked into the eyes of the sick and the young, the elderly and the weak, they, too, must have felt a sense of despair. Had they labored for three years to keep these refugees alive, only to see them die once they returned home?

As the drivers climbed into their wagons and the refugees turned their faces towards Bosnia, Adeline and Priscilla stood watching them embark, a light rain beginning to fall. But before the caravan could proceed, someone hurried towards them with a telegram from Agram: the Sava river had reached such a height that crossing was impossible; the refugees were to stay where they were until they received further orders. It was a reprieve, but not a joyous one. The Sava might not be passable until frozen over, which would mean an even colder journey and harsher conditions once they arrived.

The assembly turned in resignation, showing neither relief nor despair, and without a word returned to their quarters. Then, as if to answer the occasion, the clouds let loose a torrent of rain, pounding against the shacks where refugee families gathered to discuss their fate. It thrashed against the house where Adeline composed a letter about the days' events to be published in London, soaking the earth and making impassable the roads, creating yet one more barrier between these exiles and the home they loved, between Bosnia and her people.

By January, Adeline and Priscilla were back in Dalmatia and the repatriation of Bosnia was proceeding despite the harsh weather and unlivable conditions awaiting the refugees in their towns and villages. The end of the war, which one might imagine would have brought an end to the suffering of the refugees, only served to increase it. Because the fields were not sown the summer before, there was no corn. Even if corn could have been milled, it could not have been stored since no sufficiently dry buildings remained. The refugees, having returned to the towns from which they came, were "cowering amid the ashes of their former homes . . . almost without food, without bedding, furniture, nearly without clothes, without seed, cattle, or implements to till the ground—in shelters which scarcely deserve the name huts . . . choked with smoke, or afraid even to light a fire lest the frail erection should be burned down."[64]

The ladies, as they did countless times throughout the crisis, responded quickly, sending relief expeditions into Bosnia. The wagons, groaning beneath half a ton of ground corn and bread, repeatedly crossed the narrow mountain passageways. The life-sustaining food was distributed among the shacks, caves, and huts to which the refugees had returned. Priscilla wrote that, despite all the suffering they had witnessed over the previous three years, the "poor scarecrows" who assembled at the distributions were the "most miserable" they had yet seen, a fact even more disheartening with the knowledge that they were "the strongest and best clad of the families they represented."[65] The most heart-rending moments, though, were when they saw their former students.

Three boys who had attended one of the schools appeared at the distribution site in Strmica. Their faces were pale and bore the signs of prolonged deprivation. Approaching Priscilla, they produced carefully kept schoolbooks and showed her that they still remembered how to read. Priscilla's heart broke. In the school, they had received a daily allowance of bread and a chance to improve themselves. Looking up into her eyes, one boy asked when the school would reopen. With a quivering voice, Priscilla told him that the school was closed and would not be opening again. Another boy, so weak that he struggled to speak, pleaded with her to take them in and give them a place to live. He was orphaned and they were dying from lack of food. Priscilla wanted to say yes. However, she knew it was impossible. She could give them a supply of corn, but that was all she could do. They thanked her for the food, attempting to hide their sadness, and turned back towards the mountains. Priscilla was left to wonder if she would see them again. Would they survive two weeks until the next distribution? Would they return to Strmica alive?

From Strmica, where the only refugees who remained (about 300) were those too sick, too lame, too old, or too blind to make the return journey, the ladies continued distributing provisions every two weeks to those who were able to cross the mountains. The amount of provisions that they distributed during that winter and spring was astounding: 354,426 pounds of corn, 1,638 shovels, 1,453 pick-axes, 575 wood-cutting axes. In February alone, over 16,000 people were fed. That did not include the money they gave directly or used to purchase livestock. The Bosnian and Herzegovinian Fugitives and Orphan Relief Fund was running dry, but for this very moment the money had been raised. After sustaining the exiles for three years, how could they let them die upon reaching their own soil?

In May, they published an advertisement in England with a "special appeal for money to buy seed-corn and seeds". The ladies knew that for the agrarian Bosnians, that year's crop was perhaps the most important of their generation, which determined a new beginning or a dark end. The appeal continued, "if these are not supplied before the middle of June there will be no harvest in many districts, and consequent famine next winter."[66] That June they did, in fact, send seed to the farmers of Bosnia, ensuring a fall harvest. But they also imported something else. The summer of 1879, Adeline and Priscilla left Knin and, themselves, were repatriated to Sarajevo.

Adeline's return to Bosnia was not as simple or certain as she had hoped. To many of the 250,000 Bosnian refugees, she was a hero. The suspicions she had faced at the outset of the uprising had been replaced with veneration; doors of opportunity were open to her in villages and towns throughout the country. She had proven herself a friend of the Slavs. Adeline always considered the schools to be the most important aspect of their work. When she and Georgina first opened the institution in Sarajevo, their desire was to train schoolmistresses who could bring education to their neighbors. Less than a decade later, thanks to the refugee schools, Adeline had 24 trained and experienced teachers spread throughout the country. She had a reason to be optimistic about the future.

In the early months of 1879, Adeline financed the opening of four new schools in Bihać for children who were returning home from Slavonia. Unfortunately, the Austrian officials, wading through the murky and dangerous waters of the newly conquered territory, were not as quick to trust Adeline as the refugees were. Any sort of Slav-oriented education could threaten to reignite the recently extinguished fires. They quickly moved to suppress and close the schools.

When Adeline appealed to them in defense of the institutions, she discovered that not only her work was in jeopardy, but also her ability to return to Sarajevo. According to the authorities, there were issues to consider, papers to file and questions to answer. It seemed that the authorities preferred a Bosnia without Adeline in it. Perhaps the new government underestimated the range and influence of Adeline's friends. A group of her supporters, including Miss Nightingale, enlisted the help of Canon Henry Liddon, one of the most influential men in the Church of England, and former Prime Minister Gladstone to draft letters to Bishop Strossmayer, the Croatian Catholic Bishop of Djakovo, imploring him to intercede for Adeline. The bishop, although expressing admiration for Miss Irby, confessed that he was powerless in Bosnia and uncertain that his word would carry much weight. He concluded his letter, though, with the assurance that he would contact his more influential friends in Bosnia asking them to recommend Miss Irby and her work.

The authorities relented. Adeline was allowed to return to her school in Sarajevo.

How many obstacles had Adeline overcome up to this point? Would she be deterred by simple bureaucratic foot-dragging? Her relentless opposition to failure always resulted in the rejoicing of others: the 2,000 students wearing fresh clothes, fully fed, minds growing; the desperate mother, last hope extinguished, hearing the hoof beats of a relief expedition; the despondent young man, given a purpose for life in teaching others; the child born years later, ignorant of the uprising, alive because her parents survived. She fought so that others would know joy.

It was fitting, then, that as she packed her belongings in Knin in preparation for their return to Sarajevo, Adeline was filled with the giddy excitement of a young girl starting school. A fresh start. An unknown future. New barriers to confront. New victories to be won.

According to Adeline's accounting, from 1 October 1875 to 13 June 1879, they distributed almost £41,000 in food, clothing, shoes, housing, and education. This does not include money from their own pocket that they used to cover their expenses and advertise the fund. Of course, there are higher estimates of their expenditures. Arthur Evans, who was a key supporter of the relief work and a constant presence in the region, wrote, years later, of the £60,000 given out through the fund. Petar Mirković, who as Adeline's secretary was closest to the numbers, but as a beneficiary of her work would have ample reason to exaggerate, set the total at almost five times more. A safe estimate would be that Adeline and Priscilla spent between $3 million and $4 million (in today's equivalent) on the Bosnian people living as refugees in Dalmatia and Slavonia.

It is impossible to estimate exactly how many lives their work saved, but of the 150,000 refugees living in Croatia, surely 50,000 to 75,000 benefited in some way from their labors and tens of thousands survived directly because of it. In the town of Strmica alone, 27,000 people were fed, clothed and housed.

Perhaps more important than the tally sheet and figures, though, is the very fact that they came, they stayed, and they helped. At the end of one of the many long days of distribution, a man came up to Adeline, praising her "holy" deeds and ensuring her that the people and history would remember her good works forever. To this Adeline laughed and replied: "Support for the one inferior to you is holy. Truth is holy. History is not holy because it is full of lies, as are the people who write it. Thank you very much! What I do here is enough for me."[67]

One historian succinctly summarized what she did "here":

Along the plains of Slavonia beside the river Sava the two ladies had first shown stamina and courage; in the harsh wastes of the Dinaric Alps they had proved their fortitude. In blistering heat and in perishing cold, the distribution had gone on. When her cart was overturned in mid-stream, Miss Irby was carried to the bank ready to continue the journey. Caught in a snowstorm, she had refused to turn back; it was easier, she had insisted, to press on than for four thousand families to starve. She had descended down into the damp pits to see for herself how the cave-dwellers existed... she had slept as the honored guest in a small cottage of one room, with a fire in the middle, a cow in the corner and eighteen others sleeping around. To the refugees she had shown patience, sympathy, and understanding. Their relief went to those who needed it most. Never were those pernicious questions asked: Who are you? Why are you here? What is your faith? Where have you come from? Only one question was asked: What do you need? And it was given.[68]

ON THE WAY TO BROD

The battles that count aren't the ones for gold medals. The
struggles within yourself—the invisible, inevitable battles
inside all of us—that's where it's at.
—Jesse Owens, Gold Medal Olympic Athlete[69]

A S THE LEAVES on the hills around Sarajevo faded from green to red, the book about Adeline began to take form. After half a year's work, I had found a rhythm in the writing. On most weekday mornings, I made the short walk down the hill into Baščaršija just as shop owners arrived to open their stores. In the stillness of that hour, my mind filled with stories of Adeline. The problems I wrestled the day before were often answered while walking. At the bakery across the street from the Sebilj I bought a pastry—the smell of the freshly baked bread awakening my senses—and set out for a coffee shop.

Mornings were perfect for writing; the coffee shops of Baščaršija were relatively empty and a quiet corner was easy to find. On warm days, I sat outside at a small café that was tucked away on a side street. There among the potted trees and brightly colored umbrellas I found inspiration. On wet or cold days, I hid myself among the shelves of a local bookstore. I supposed that the presence of books would help me create one. A good morning would go by in a flash. Around noon I packed up my notes and moved on with my day.

While the book was progressing, my language study was not. I found an inverse relationship between good days writing and good days speaking Bosnian. In order to correct that problem, my wife and I decided to take a langauge immersion weekend. On a Friday in November, we loaded the kids in the car and left Sarajevo to spend the weekend with a family in Doboj, a town two hours to the north.

As we drove along E73, I thought about Adeline. We were driving the same route she took many times, the north-south road from Sarajevo to the border at Bosanski Brod. With a car, we could reach the border in three hours. Adeline needed two days to make the 140 mile journey in the Austrian post cart. I tried to imagine traveling six miles an hour seated on a bale of hay. I tried to picture the landscape as it was before the land was cleared for towns and roads. I tried to see Bosnia as Adeline must have seen it: clean, rushing rivers; colorful, green mountains; vibrant, natural beauty. I rolled down the window and tried to hear Bosnia as Adeline must have heard it: the melodic chirping of birds, the rhythmic rattling of the cart, the hypnotic rustling of the wind through the leaves. The two-hour drive passed quickly.

In Doboj, we threw ourselves into the language. We were staying with a family we had met a few months earlier on the coast. They had two children—a boy and a girl—who played well with our kids and Taylor and I got along well with the parents too. None of them spoke English. It was the perfect immersion opportunity.

The night we arrived, we sat around the coffee table in their living room while the children played.

"So, is there anything new in your life?" the wife asked.

"Actually, there is," Taylor answered, looking at me with a smile. "But, I will let Izzy tell you." Taylor called our four-year-old daughter in from the other room. "Izzy, is there anything special that you want to announce?"

"Yes," she replied shyly in her cute Bosnian. Then, more loudly, she exclaimed, "I am going to have a new brother or sister!"

"Really!" Our hosts looked at both of us, first for confirmation and then as congratulation. "That is wonderful!"

Izzy beamed like a proud older sister. Our children were impatiently awaiting the baby's arrival. Each morning they would climb into Taylor's lap and plead, "Is the baby coming today, mommy?" Taylor would gently remind them that the baby wouldn't be ready until June, to which they would respond, "Mommy, is June tomorrow?"

Our friends in Sarajevo were just as excited as our children. Although each friend reacted differently to the news, there was always some combination of shouting, hugging, and celebrating. Taylor and I were also happy. The day we saw the baby's heartbeat at the doctor's office was extraordinary. A little life was growing, one that we would soon be able to hold.

The rest of the weekend was filled with conversations over coffee, strolls around the town, and games of chase in the park. On Sunday afternoon we left Doboj for home.

We decided to take a detour on the return trip in order to visit a shopping center in the town of Vitez. The store was one enormous room the size of five soccer fields. As far as the eye could see there was row after row of high-quality, low-priced goods. Knowing that the kids would not survive two hours of shopping, I took them upstairs to the play area while Taylor— wide-eyed with excitement—headed in the direction of the kitchen supplies.

Eventually, Taylor called to let me know that she was wait- ing in line to pay. The kids and I went downstairs and played on the plastic helicopter ride just beyond the cashier. As soon as I saw Taylor walking towards me I knew something was wrong. Her eyes were red and her face was taut as if holding back tears. I asked her what was wrong. She told me that some- thing was not right with the baby. Leaving the cart with me, she rushed into the bathroom. My heart sank. *What could be wrong with the baby? We just saw the heartbeat last week?*

When she returned, I could tell she had been crying. We stepped a few feet away from the helicopter where the children were still playing and she told me that she had started bleeding. We were both afraid.

In the car we assessed the situation. Most likely, the baby was fine. Strange things were normal during pregancy. A little blood didn't mean that the baby was in danger. The rest of the way home we tried to distract ourselves with conversation.

The next morning we went to the doctor. The waiting room felt colder than it had the week before. The flourescent lights seemed to expose our insecurities. We were frightened, but do- ing our best to stay hopeful. The nurse called Taylor back to the examination room. She lay down on the light blue bed and the doctor turned on the ultrasound machine. The familiar black and grey image flashed onto the screen, but there was no heart- beat. Our baby was no longer alive.

★ ★ ★

The month following the miscarriage was like a deep, dark hole in the earth. Taylor went through a cycle of emotions—anger, blame, depression, sadness—as her body recovered. Although I wasn't under the influence of shifting hormones, I experienced those emotions too. Izzy was asking hard questions: what happened to the baby, why is mommy so sad, where is the baby now? Elijah, also too young to understand, still climbed up into Taylor's lap and asked, "When is the baby coming out, mommy?" It was a difficult time to be so far away from family. Our Sarajevo friends, however, were kind and understanding. Many of them descended into the pit with us just to put an arm around our shoulders. Comfort, though, only dulled the sadness, but it could not take it away. Only time could do that.

The book came to a standstill. Whatever time I had, I gave to Taylor and the kids. When I sat down to write, no words came to mind. The dark shadows of depression had clouded out the light of creativity. At times, I wondered if it was even worth the effort. But as fall turned into winter, the shadows lifted. I began to write again. The light of Adeline's life seemed to shine even brighter, walking out of the valley of the shadow of death.

Pouring myself back into the book, I began to see gaps in my research. There were resources I needed to find in order to understand Adeline and her motivation. Fortunately, I had help. George, the student I had reconnected with at the success lecture, had become one of my closest friends. That first year in Sarajevo, we met three to four times a week for coffee. One morning he called me with good news: he found something I really wanted to see.

I rushed over to the Historical Archive of Sarajevo where he had been searching for articles about Adeline's funeral. When I entered the front door, George was standing in the lobby with a big grin on his face.

"We hit the jackpot," he exclaimed, before I even had a chance to take off my coat.

George led me into the reading room, which was small, with a large table in the center and maps lining the walls. On one side of the room there were bookshelves rising up to the ceiling. Through a door, left slightly ajar, I could see a second room full of mobile shelving—the heart of the archive. He pointed to the faded and torn periodicals stacked on the table.

"Eighty pages just on Miss Irby," he declared. "It is all from 1934. There was a celebration for the 100th anniversary of her birth."

I picked up the aged documents and started flipping through the pages. There was article after article about Adeline. There were also pictures. I studied the photo of her school, the first one I had ever found. I could almost see the girls skipping across the courtyard and bounding through the front door. There was also a photo reproduction of a painting of Adeline towards the end of her life. The heavy lines on her face be-trayed her age, but her head was still held high. She was noble until the end.

The lady who worked in the archive walked over to where I was sitting. "Is this what you were looking for?" she asked.

"This is better than what I was looking for. Who would have thought that the archive would have so many historical docu-ments," I added jokingly.

"Have you seen Miss Irby's fund?"

"Yes, I know about her fund," I replied, still engrossed in the documents in front of me. On my computer at home I had over 100 newspaper articles from England written about or by Adeline. Among those were advertisements for her refugee relief fund.

"Let me know if you need anything," the lady mentioned over her shoulder as she returned to her desk.

George and I spent another 30 minutes looking over the documents, verifying that we had photocopied everything important. We loaded the copies in my bag, put on our coats, and prepared to leave. Before walking out the door, I asked the lady, who was still at her desk, if she knew of any other places where we could find articles on Adeline.

"You mean besides the fund we have here? There is the National Archives in the Presidency building. Have you looked there?"

"We have an appointment there for next week, but..." Something about the way she said 'fund' made me wonder if I had understood her in our previous conversation. "What do you mean by 'the fund you have here.'"

"We keep a fund of letters and documents relating to Miss Irby."

"You have letters?" I blurted out.

"Yes, of course," she responded calmly and disappeared into the second room. A moment later she returned with a thick folder. "Here, you can look through this."

Not even taking time to remove our coats, we sat in front of the folder and started unwinding the string that held it closed. Pulling back the cover we found a stack of papers, four inches high. The sheet on top was a handwritten note in German, penned with strong, confident strokes. Knowing only a little

German, I was unable to make out the message, but the numbers throughout gave it the feel of a business letter. I turned it over. There, clearly inscribed at the end of the note, was the signature of the author: A. P. Irby. I was holding a letter from Adeline.

Reading books about Adeline was one thing, exploring the country she lived in was another, but holding something she held was an entirely new experience. It was like a doorway opened between my time and hers.

George looked at me in disbelief. "Forget what I said earlier. *This* is the jackpot."

We started dividing the letters between us, gingerly handling the aged corners. As I passed a set to George, a small, white card fell loose onto the table. It was the exact size of a modern business card and looked to be the same texture. The card was unmarked. I picked it up, feeling the weight and quality of the paper between my fingers, and turned it over. On the opposite side, typed across the center of the card, was a name: Adeline Paulina Irby. It was Adeline's calling card.

I nudged George and held the card so he could read it. His eyes widened with surprise. He glanced at me, and then looked back at the card. We both sat in silence. It was like meeting Miss Irby in a tangible way. George put his arm around my shoulder and gave me a pat on the back. Nothing else needed to be said.

THE FLOWERS OF BOSNIA

1878-1881

Judge each day not by the harvest you reap
but by the seeds you plant.
—Robert Louis Stevenson, Scottish author

I have many beautiful flowers," he said; "but the children are
the most beautiful flowers of all.
—Oscar Wilde, from *The Selfish Giant*

A T THE WESTERN entrance to Sarajevo, on a main thoroughfare leading into Baščaršija, stood a two-story building, four-square and solid, rising conspicuously above its smaller, Turkish-styled neighbors. Behind the building, which many called the *Zavod*, a tree-filled garden stretched downward to the bank of the Miljacka River. In front of it rose a hillside that displayed, on seasonal rotation, the natural beauty of the year: first blanketed in white; then dotted with primrose and violets; then carpeted, soft and green; then bursting with purple crocus and cyclamens, red and golden leaves, and scarlet hips.

From the summer of 1878 through the summer of 1879 the *Zavod* survived at least two threats to its existence. In August 1878, as General Filipović led the Austro-Hungarian troops towards Sarajevo to establish Hapsburg rule, a hastily gathered retinue of Sarajevans, representing each of the ethnic and religious groups, mustered a defense. The invading army needed only a day to raise their yellow and black flag in victory. As the soldiers entered the town, any house that was suspected of resistance was burned. The *Zavod* was taken as military barracks.

The next year, a merchant named Schwarz was doing metalwork on an August evening when, coming too close to a barrel with the fire, he set his workshop ablaze. Aided by strong winds, the fire rapidly spread from house to house, shop to shop, igniting wooden structures stripped of moisture by the long, hot summer. Down into the valley from Latinluk it raged, swallowing up the entire western end of Baščaršija, laying to waste 434 small workshops, 304 houses, 135 buildings, 36 roads, and filling the air with the acrid smell of ash. Beneath the smoke and floating embers, the *Zavod* remained. Only a month earlier, the Austrian soldiers had withdrawn to a different barracks and the owners returned to transform the building back to its original purpose. Instead of the gruff tones of military men, the garden was filled with the laughter of children at play. Exactly ten years earlier, on a cloudless August afternoon in the presence of a hundred witnesses, including all six European consuls and their families, the *Zavod* had been dedicated as a place of security and enlightenment, growth and opportunity. Girls would come there from the poorest areas of Bosnia and grow to become trained schoolmistresses taking education back to their villages. If Adeline had her way, the *Zavod* would become that place once again.

The *Zavod*, which before the uprising seemed a substantial if not oversized space for the school and its 12 students, was now pressed to its limits. The five girls who had been sent to Prague at the outset of the war returned, rejoining the handful of pupils who had remained in Sarajevo with the caretaker and his wife; added to them were some of the refugee children and orphans from the schools in Slavonia and Dalmatia. There were 66 children in all. No longer simply a training school for girls, the *Zavod* was a home, an orphanage, an industrial training center, a school, and a nursery. The youngest "student" was a one-year-old baby girl; and of the 66 children, 41 were boys.

In order to accommodate all of the children, Adeline purchased an old Turkish house nearby as a boys' residence and placed them under the care of an older, widowed woman. As the ladies had done in their refugee schools, they worked to find apprenticeships for the boys and, within two years, they had found jobs across Bosnia for all but eight who remained to attend a day school in town. One of those who remained was a 20-year-old who, as a refugee, had been housed in Plavno. Only a few years earlier as one of many homeless, hungry, haggard exiles scrapping for survival amidst the snowdrifts of the Dinarite, he was unsure of his future, or if he would even have one. In Sarajevo, he became a model and an encouragement to the other younger boys when he received a post at the Customs Department from which he earned a living wage.

As for the girls, by 1881, the training school was again taking shape. That summer Margaret, the wife of Arthur Evans, came for an extended visit to the school and, on her return to England, published a thorough report of the day-to-day activities there. The picture Margaret painted was one of industry and spirituality, discipline and joy, education of the mind and development of the heart.

At six each morning a large bell rang and the day began. The children dressed and went about their morning chores. The school only kept one indoor servant, so aside from the cooking, most of the household tasks were done by the children: serving and cleaning up after meals; sweeping and scrubbing the floors; making, mending and washing the clothes; cow-tending and gardening; carrying in the water and wood. Twice a week the *Zavod* was cleaned from top to bottom and occasionally, when the cook was ill, the children would even take over the preparation of meals, which was no small order with 43 mouths to feed. By participating in the upkeep of the school, the children were developing not only their character, but also valuable skills that they could take back with them to their villages.

By 7:45 AM, all the work was done and the children assembled for morning prayers. Each day the children would read a chapter from the Bible, verse by verse, taking turns reading each one; then they would sing a hymn and read a prayer. The children loved to sing. The hymns were mostly

well-known English tunes—Margaret mentioned "Abide with
Me", "Jesus, Lover of My Soul", and "Rock of Ages"—with the
words translated into the local language. These songs that
were written by wealthy Englishmen thousands of miles away,
rang true for the students whose lives were marked by the
horrors of war. Often lines from these hymns, such as the one
below, echoed around the garden:

> *Other refuge have I none,*
> *Hangs my helpless soul on Thee;*
> *Leave, ah! leave me not alone,*
> *Still support and comfort me.*
> *All my trust on Thee is stayed,*
> *All my help from Thee I bring;*
> *Cover my defenseless head*
> *With the shadow of Thy wing.*

To close the morning devotional, one child was chosen to
recite the Lord's Prayer:

> *Our Father, which art in heaven,*
> *hallowed be thy name;*
> *thy kingdom come;*
> *thy will be done,*
> *on earth as it is in heaven.*
> *Give us this day our daily bread.*
> *And forgive us our trespasses,*
> *as we forgive them that trespass against us.*
> *And lead us not into temptation;*
> *but deliver us from evil.*
> *For thine is the kingdom,*

the power, and the glory,
for ever and ever.
Amen.

School lasted for five hours each weekday and included reading, writing, mathematics, history, literature, and, now that Bosnia was under the Hapsburg's rule, German. Margaret noted that the students "are very affectionate, warm hearted children... sharper and less shy and awkward than most English children of the same class."[70] Adeline and Priscilla infused the school with a love of learning by continuing to grow themselves. Besides speaking Serbo-Croatian fluently, Adeline taught herself Italian, French, and German, could understand Russian, and would often read books in Greek, Latin and Ancient Hebrew. In this environment, the children responded with eagerness and passion, understanding the opportunity granted them and not wanting it to pass them by.

The *Zavod* was also a happy and bright place where hard work and joy lived side-by-side. The children loved to roam the hillside opposite the school, taking in the view of the valley below and returning home with arms full of freshly picked flowers. On clear days, the girls spent their free time in the garden singing or dancing the traditional *kolo* or playing some of the English games they had learned. Sunday was a day of rest and spiritual refreshment. After an hour of hymn-singing there would be a short lesson from the Bible then the girls would go to their own churches for the service.

Although Adeline allowed the children to remain under the spiritual care of their priests, she did not abdicate her responsibility for their spiritual growth. She was fond of asking them what passages had been read at the service, discussing the text with them, and encouraging them to study it on their own. She used the Bible to address moral issues—hypocrisy, vanity, selfishness, greed, and other vices—as well as emotional issues—loneliness, hopelessness, helplessness, insecurity, and pain. God, she taught the children, was their comforter, their protector, their deliverer; He was all-powerful, all-knowing, and holy; there was no one else worthy of their prayers, their worship or their trust. Most Sundays during the warmer months, groups of children would gather under the shade in the garden, Bibles in hand, the older reading to the younger.

In many ways, the *Zavod* felt like a large family. While Margaret was visiting, two new children arrived from Slavonia where their mother was a widowed schoolmistress. The younger of the two, a four-year-old named Mileta, was crying uncontrollably, distraught from having to leave her mother. She was gently handed over to an 11-year-old student, who was instructed to act as little Mileta's "mother" at the school. Within a few days, she was out and about in the garden, smiling, laughing and clinging to her "mother's" dress.

Many of these same children who cried coming into the school, cried upon their departure. They were leaving their family for a second time. One young woman wrote a letter to Adeline expressing her sadness at saying goodbye to the school:

> *It is hard for me to say goodbye to this dear house in which I knew no sorrow nor poverty. I was happy. I have a Father in Heaven and my mother is The Noble. I'm losing everything now but my dear*

*Father in Heaven to whom I always pray and hope
He will be there for me forever, be my guardian.
Today I can see that I am poor, as I leave my beloved benefactress. The Noble did me more good
and saw more of the bad done to me than my own
mother, whom I don't even remember. Let the dear
Lord make it up to her, I will pray and I will not
forget her till the day I die. I tell you again dear
friend, with sadness in my heart I think of leaving
this house, and it's hard to think I will never see
my good and beloved Noble again.*[71]

The *Zavod* was an extension and reflection of Adeline. The
school was industrious and focused, an institution in which
young lives could be molded into useful and upstanding con-
tributors to society. Adeline once wrote to a student who was
studying abroad:

*You are now in the foreign land. The world is a
very big book. You can learn a lot of nice and
good things from that book, which will be useful to you in life. Yes, you will be able to see very
dirty pages of that book as well. Watch out for
those dirty pages, so that your hands and your
soul don't become corrupt; because what follows
is the downfall of that nice species called man. Go
through the clean and pure pages of that book,
learn good examples and use them. This time I
am sending you a book called Character. I have
read it and I have seen what kind of jewelry a
man should wear, that is, to be a man—character,*

bright character! Hurry, get your work there done,
and come back home.[72]

This was no less of a standard—character, purity, use-fulness—than what Adeline held herself to. She would dart about the *Zavod*: first in the classroom and then quickly out to the stable; a stop by the garden and then on to the kitchen; up to the bedrooms to see the children, then on to her own room to read and write. This same drive and determination which brought her to the Balkans initially, that motivated her to start the school, that sustained her through the uprising (and sustained the thousands she helped) was one of the key things she wanted to impart to the students. And because of this character, people called her *Plemenita* (The Noble).

That was not her only pseudonym, though. Petar Mirković described her as "serious and determined," but he also noted that "when she spoke she would smile." Because of her pleasant smile the students began calling her *Vesela* (Cheerful). Nothing could more quickly interrupt Adeline's determined path around the *Zavod* than the sight (or sound) of the children singing and dancing. She would find a seat, no longer *Plemenita* but *Vesela*, and with rapture watch the joyous celebration of life. She loved the children like they were her own. She was their *Vesela* and they were, to her, the beauty and hope of Bosnia.

While still in Knin during the uprising, Adeline made a trip to the home of a merchant with whom she had some unfinished business. Upon arriving at the house and discovering that the businessman was not at home, she accepted the kind invitation of his wife to sit for a coffee. The lady brought Adeline out to the garden where she began to proudly show off, one by one, her flowers.

"What do you think of my flower garden?" the merchant's wife asked Adeline.

"They are truly beautiful."

"Well, I wish that you could have seen my favorite rose. Unfortunately, despite all of my efforts, it died last winter. That rose was simply astonishing," the lady said, "the most beautiful in the whole region."

"You have a wonderful garden," Adeline replied kindly, "but the type of flowers you are growing are not, in my opinion, the most noble kind." Adeline paused to let her words register. "You may be surprised, but I also have a flower garden, and my flowers, I have to tell you, are even more beautiful than yours."

"Well," replied the lady, a little taken aback and yet simultaneously curious, "I will just have to come for a visit so that you can show them to me. If they are as wonderful as you say, maybe I can take some back with me for my garden."

"I would be delighted. I think that my flowers, which are a special breed from the mountains of Bosnia and Herzegovina, would be a fine addition to your garden."

At that moment, the merchant arrived home. Adeline excused herself, concluded her business and returned home.

Not long afterwards, the lady came to see Adeline. At the end of her visit, as she was preparing to leave, she remembered their conversation about the flowers.

"Oh," the lady exclaimed, "I almost forgot. Please, if it is not too much trouble, let me see your flower garden before I leave."

"Yes, gladly!" Adeline answered. "Just come with me and I will show them to you one by one."

The two ladies walked into the neighboring room where 20 children, ages three to seven, were quietly playing. The kids rushed over to Adeline, grabbing at her clothes, kissing her hands, as she gently stroked their heads.

"Madam, this is my flower garden," Adeline said, gesturing towards the cleanly dressed orphans around her. "And each flower has its own story."

"Vuka" Adeline called out to one of the children, "come here."

A little girl about seven years old came over and climbed up in Adeline's lap.

"This flower is called Vuka. When she was found on the Dinara mountain, at the spring for the river Cetina, she was living alone in the woods without food, barely alive and barely speaking. The people who found her brought her to me. The poor girl was only skin and bone stuck together; her eyes had sunken into her head and she could barely look or move about. Had she come a few days later, she would not have survived. It was very hard to bring her back. I was very careful while raising her." Adeline paused, looking up at the rest of the children. "And each one of these flowers has their own story."

The lady, who had by now gotten over the initial shock of finding the "garden" full of children, sat quietly, staring at Vuka.

"I promised that you could take a couple flowers home for your own garden," Adeline continued. "Please, feel free to pick whichever ones you want."

The merchant's wife left with three of Adeline's "flowers"; with her they found a home, a family, a place where they could grow.

In their big "garden" in Sarajevo, the *Zavod*, Adeline and Priscilla were growing "flowers" to brighten and color Bosnia and Herzegovina. This was the original work Adeline and Georgina began and this was the important work Adeline and Priscilla continued. For them, "to promote the education of girls and to raise the status of women in Bosnia and the Herzegovina,"[73] was even more significant than their response during the refugee crisis. What could be more important to a nation than the development of young people: nurturing their minds, enhancing their skills, maturing their convictions and forming their character?

This work, however, was difficult. The years of the uprising, although draining, were full of excitement: emergency fundraising meetings, letters printed in *The Times*, supplies bought by the thousands, appeals by distinguished supporters, growing fame and recognition. Now, words like "urgent", "immediate", and "desperate" were replaced by the long, slow, repetitive march of education. Refugee work had also been immediately fulfilling. They could see the direct results of their labor: a sick child well, a hungry family fed, a homeless widow sheltered. The shaping of young minds, however, cannot be easily measured on a balance sheet or reported in an update. With education, many years of sowing precede the harvest. That is why Florence Nightingale called the *Zavod* "a

MEETING MISS IRBY

little higher and more difficult work"[74] than even what they
had accomplished in Dalmatia and Slavonia. For almost four
years they had kept people alive. Now they were teaching
them how to truly live.

The Nobel Prize winner Ivo Andrić said of Adeline, "We
will never be able to completely find out or assess all that
this woman has done for Bosnia... because everything that
she did, she did with the greatest of sacrifices, without praise
and glory." Numbers cannot tell the tale. Throughout Bosnia
and Herzegovina, beautiful flowers were transplanted from
Adeline's garden, growing bright and colorful like the crocus
and primrose on the hillside across from the *Zavod*, spreading, wherever they were planted, "the love for their country,
their home and work, and the wish for a better, more noble
living."[75]

THE SPARK OF ETERNAL LOVE

The spark of eternal love, which God had placed upon her soul,
flamed at the aisle of love toward the neighbor, in fire, which
Charity and education would continue to keep and encourage.
In spirit she stands in the middle of these yards...
and yells to you: "Go and do good!"
—Speech at Adeline's Funeral

Thou, O Christ, art all I want
More than all in thee I find!
Raise the fallen, cheer the faint,
Heal the sick, and lead the blind;
Just and holy is thy name,
I am all unrighteousness;
False and full of sin I am,
Thou art full of truth and grace.

Plenteous grace with thee is found,
Grace to cover all my sin,
Let the healing streams abound;

Make and keep me pure within:
Thou of life the fountain art,
Freely let me take of thee,
Spring thou up within my heart,
Rise to all eternity.
—"Jesus, Lover of my Soul," song sung at Adeline's
schools

A CAFÉ IN Sarajevo stands directly across the street from the land Adeline once owned. The building that used to be her school has been replaced by a larger structure, and the garden is now an open courtyard surrounded by four story apartment buildings. The café is one of the trendier ones in town; it is always full of young, fashionable Sarajevans slowly enjoying their Italian espressos. I often sit outside and imagine the scene as it was over a century ago: bustling, joyous, and full of life; songs drifting through the open windows; groups of children sitting beneath the trees in the garden; the Miljacka passing by the edge of the yard. It was at this cafe that Slavko and I met for coffee on a sunny but cold February morning.

From a distance, Slavko looks a bit intimidating: tall, well-fed, black hair, dark eyes and full goatee, black leather jacket. Not exactly the kind of guy you'd want to run into in a dark alley—at least, in appearance. Twenty years ago, when he was nineteen, he started working at the casino in his hometown of Mostar. The job brought him a good paycheck (especially for the standards of Yugoslavia in the late-1980s) but also initiated him into the world of organized crime. He quickly progressed in the organization until he was managing three local casinos. Around that time, he started spending time with a beautiful girl from Mostar named Sanja who was perfect in every way except one. She was religious. Slavko was a staunch atheist and loyal communist party member. For him there was no need for religion. He told Sanja that he wanted to date her, but only if she met his conditions. First, she had to throw out the cross earrings that she wore every day. Second, she had to stop going to church. This, of course, is ironic since Slavko is now the pastor of one of the 30 or so Protestant Christian churches in Bosnia and Herzegovina.

I had invited him to coffee because I had some questions about the connection between the Protestant faith and humanitarian work, something that Slavko has been involved with for over a decade. To the degree that Slavko is intimidating from a distance, he is disarming in conversation. He laughs openly, jokes freely, talks loudly and his eyes brighten when the topic turns to something he is passionate about.

"What kind of humanitarian work is your church involved in?" I asked, taking a sip of my macchiato.

"Well," he began, "this past Christmas we distributed 600 packages to children in our neighborhood on Koševsko Brdo and at a school just outside of Sarajevo. Each year the members of our church put on a free puppet show and every child who attends gets a shoebox of gifts. We also have ongoing humanitarian aid. One of our members, who is a doctor, volunteers part of her time each week so we can offer free medical care to the public. There are also 20 families who receive packages of food from us every month."

"Twenty families? Your church is not that big, is it?" I asked.

"No, we have ten families."

"So you, as a church, are regularly helping twice as many people as are in the church. Why do you do humanitarian work? Couldn't you use those resources just for the people in the church?"

"Well, we do help people who are a part of our church, but we think it is important to meet the needs of everyone we can. There is a saying, 'Do not do to others what you do not want them to do to you.' I think that is too easy. It is passive. It means that as long as I am not doing something bad to someone else I am ok. But this is actually a distortion of what Jesus said in the Bible: 'Do to others what you would have them do to you.' This is more active. If you were hungry, wouldn't you want someone to give you food?" he finished, his voice deep and clear.

Slavko understood hunger. In 1992, when the war broke out in Mostar, he and his family were stuck in a hopeless situation. His brother-in-law began going to the various aid organizations looking for food to feed his family. At each office he was handed a form that asked for his name, contact information, and nationality. Because of his brother-in-law's answer to the nationality question, he was repeatedly denied help. He had to return home to his wife and children empty-handed. Then Slavko's mother heard about an organization called Agape, named for the Greek word meaning "unconditional love." When she came to apply and they asked for her grandchildren's birth certificates she expected another rejection. To her surprise, the worker just glanced at the documents, confirmed that she did in fact have grandchildren, and handed her a box of food.

"Jesus fed people who were hungry," Slavko continued, leaning forward intensely with his elbows on his knees. "He healed people who were sick. But that was not the most important thing to Jesus. One time Jesus got into a conversation with a woman who had come out to a well to draw water. He told her that the water from the well would satisfy her thirst, but only for a little while, and then she would have to come and get more; but, that he could give her a kind of water that, if she drank it, would take away her thirst forever. He was speaking figuratively about quenching her thirst for a real, spiritual connection with God. Physical needs were important to Jesus, but he was much more concerned with people's spiritual needs. He is the one who said, 'What do you benefit if you gain the whole world but lose your soul?'"

Slavko paused a moment, looking out the window at the big yellow building where Adeline once housed orphan children. "We give people food," he continued, "because they need help. The physical aid is not dependent on them agreeing with us. But, my greatest desire is that people will come to experience the unconditional love, forgiveness, and acceptance that God offers through Jesus in the Bible. I know what it is like to feel alienated from God, and I do not wish that on anyone."

The first time Slavko ever prayed was not long after the war started. The conflict had left him confused and helpless; this was a problem that his usual tools—connections, friends, and money—could not fix. With a Croatian mother and a Serbian father, what choice could he make that would not put him fighting against someone he loved? One night, he and Sanja were walking through town when they passed by a church. Sanja asked if she could go in to pray; Slavko reluctantly agreed, planning to stay outside and wait for her. Something, that night, compelled him to follow her into the church. He stood alone at the back of the sanctuary unsure how to pray. Eventually he just said what came to his mind, "God, if you exist, please help me." After that he recited a list of promises that he would fulfill if God came through for him. Then they left the sanctuary.

God did come through for them. Through inexplicable circumstances, they made it safely out of the country. Slavko, though, forgot about his promises; not much changed in his life. In exile, he and Sanja married and made the most of their uprooted lives.

After the war, they moved to Belgrade, found jobs, and started a family. It was the birth of their first child that forced Slavko to think about God again. When Jovana was born she showed signs of cerebral palsy. On their first visit to the specialist, the doctor examined her and concluded that the diagnosis was clear: Jovana was a textbook example of the disease. Just to be certain, the doctor ordered a series of tests to begin on the following visit. That night Slavko went into his room and prayed to God. For two weeks he prayed as his little daughter underwent one assessment after another—ultrasound brain scan, EEG, needles, big machines. When they met with the specialist a second time, the doctor was visibly upset. She looked at the results, then re-examined Jovana, looked at the results again, then re-examined their baby daughter. Finally, the doctor asked them to sit down. The specialist said that she had made mistakes before in her practice but never one as big as this. Jovana did not have cerebral palsy.

To Slavko, that was a direct answer to his prayers. A shift took place in Slavko's heart; he began to read the Bible and his life began to change. Eventually, he decided he did believe in God and would follow him whatever that meant for his life.

Slavko and Sanja had sworn never to return to Bosnia and Herzegovina. In Belgrade, they were living in an all-expenses-paid apartment. One of Slavko's wealthy relatives—his father's elderly cousin who had no children of her own—had promised to support them financially if they stayed in Belgrade to care for her and her husband. Both Slavko and Sanja were working jobs, but the rent money helped them survive. In addition to that, this relative had promised to pass on all of her inheritance to them when she died. That included the 4500 square foot villa with a half-acre garden in the exclusive Dedinje neighborhood of Belgrade as well as the weekend house on Zlatibor.

They were happy in Belgrade, yet Slavko began to feel that God wanted them to go back to Mostar. They were faced with a difficult decision: Did they stay in the comfort and financial security of Serbia, or did they do what God wanted them to do? The conversation with Slavko's relative went as they expected: stay and they could have everything; leave and they would get nothing. Not long afterwards, they moved to Mostar. Slavko started volunteering with Agape, the humanitarian organization there that had helped his family during the war, and was soon in charge of delivering food to families on both sides of the ethnically divided city.

Eventually, his path led him to Sarajevo where he, Sanja, Jovana and their youngest son David now live. Recently, Jovana won an international competition for rhythmic gymnastics. Slavko attributes all of this to the work of God in his life.

* ★ ★

The café was beginning to fill up as we came to the end of our conversation, the noise was so great that both Slavko and I were sitting at the edge of our seats, perched out over the small knee-high table, straining to hear each other. "What motivates you," I asked, coming at last to the question that most intrigued me, "to help people who are different from you—people who, as a rule, disagree with you and what you believe?"

"My faith," he answered. "My faith is my main motivation. It tells me that we are all God's creations and that we have value simply because God loved us enough to make us. But we all experience separation from God because we are not faithful to him like He is to us. We disobey him. We sin. I know and can speak from personal experience. I was a liar, a robber, a blasphemer. At first, I did not even care what God thought; then, when I did, I made all these promises that I could never keep in my own strength. Finally, I realized that it is an impossible job to be good enough for God. I cannot help myself; I need help. When I came to that conclusion, God started to change me, and he is changing me still. He is changing me so that I can help others."

Then, pausing as if struck by the truth of his own words, his eyes now bright like the crisp clear day, he concluded. "Did God wait until I was like Him before he helped me? No. I was sinful and ungodly; in fact, I was His enemy. I was against God. But, Jesus, who had no reason to love me, came into our world to be mistreated and cursed and killed, so that I could have my deepest need met, my spiritual need for a relationship with God. If Jesus sacrificed his life for me, what sacrifice is too big for me to give? It sure makes giving a box of food to a hungry family look small," he said and laughed with a shrug. "If God loved me while I was his enemy, how could I not love my neighbor just because he is different than me?"

HOME

1882-1911

Kuća bez djevojke—proljeće bez cvijeća.
(A home without girls—spring without flowers).
—Bosnian Proverb

EVERY YEAR NEW girls arrived at the *Zavod* and every year young women departed. After only a few years, Adeline and Priscilla had settled into the steady rhythm of school life—hour-by-hour, day-by-day, week-by-week, season-by-season. Within the walls of the *Zavod* life was constant and secure, but outside, the city of Sarajevo was transforming.

Wrapped in green since its founding in the 15th century, the city was now being painted with the yellow and black brushstrokes of the Hapsburg Empire. Benjamin Kallay, who from 1882 orchestrated many of the changes, believed that his mission was to "civilize Bosnia-Hercegovina" and transform it into an "enlightened European state and society."[76] This *westernization* was apparent throughout Sarajevo. In

architecture, three and four story European-style buildings were replacing the one-story wooden structures of the
Ottoman period; major religious and government structures
were built along the valley, extending the town's center towards the *Zavod*; the wall along the Miljacka was extended
to prevent seasonal flooding. In society, a growing number of
European ex-patriots filled the streets, moving quickly about
their business as civil servants, government contractors, and
merchants. Public activities such as theaters, concerts, and
cafe nightlife began to replace smaller social gatherings in
homes and religious institutions. German began to supplant
Turkish as a second language. In transpor-tation, a horse-
drawn tramline was opened on New Year's Day in 1885, and
later extended along the bank of the Miljacka; train tracks
were laid from Sarajevo through Zenica and on to Brod, effectively connecting the city to the rest of Europe.

Bosnia was pulled westward. It still maintained much of
its Ottoman heritage—handmade crafts were still fashioned
and sold in Baščaršija, veiled women still walked the cobblestone streets, minarets still called out the Ezan, groups of
men still sat squat-legged drinking coffee—but Bosnia was
no longer the entranceway to the east. In fact, it was quickly
becoming a doorway to Europe. Yet, amidst all this transformation, Adeline and Priscilla continued their labor relatively
unchanged.

In 1882, when the railway line to Brod was completed, it
was possible to reach England from Sarajevo in only four
days. After years of making the long slow journey across the
mainland of Europe, this new connection came too late for
Adeline. As each year passed, she found fewer and fewer reasons to return to London. In Sarajevo, she was already home.

*   *   *

The same year that the train line reached Sarajevo, Adeline purchased an orchard on a hillside two and a half hours outside of the city. The need for rest had been one of the main reasons she had made the long trip back to England each summer. In London she could avoid the stifling heat of the Sarajevo valley and enjoy the more comfortable company of friends and family. But, after 1882, she discovered that she could revive from the stresses of the growing city in the cool shade of the orchard's apple and plum trees. By cart, she would travel to the west along the river, eventually leaving the plain and heading uphill along a narrow path that reminded her of an English country lane; limbs of acorned oaks and wild apple trees stretched out above her head. Eventually the road, which doubled as an impromptu river in the spring, would give out and she would complete her journey on foot.

As Adeline described it:

> The place had its own romantic beauty. It was on the slope of a hill-range, looking over the Sarajevsko Polje (the plain of Sarajevo)—which then lay shimmering in rich autumn sunshine— away past the hot sulfur springs of Ilidža, to the blue green forest mountain of Igman, beneath which are the sources of the Bosna, rising at once from many springs, a broad strong river at its birth. Fronting, in the distance, higher mountain ranges; noticeably the white crags and masses of Bjelašnica, so named for the whiteness of its higher steeps and rifts which bear in the sunlight the

*semblance of eternal snow. Nearer, on the left, the
broken massy slopes of Trebević, winning at last
an almost spirey summit, pointing upwards and
skywards away from the city beneath.*[77]

She purchased the 30-acre property (which she later expanded to 40 acres) from a young man who was eager to sell
due to a particular problem with the land. This problem was
not at all related to the orchard, which produced "gold and
purple plums, russet and rosy apples and pears" in abun-
dance, had a cool breeze even on the hottest days, and contained a spring that, according to the neighbors, could cure
the fever. The problem was the tenant who refused to release any of the yield to the owner. When the owner visited his property, the tenant would chase him off with a freshly sharpened ax. Adeline, perhaps seeing an opportunity to
learn about the land tenant laws of the country or simply
recognizing a favorable financial situation, bought the land
anyway.

What Adeline did next revealed a great deal about her per-
sonality and character. First, there was justice. Invoking the
laws laid out by the Austrian administration and with the
force of their officials, she obliged the tenant to pay his right-
ful dues. She collected her share, as the landowner, plus a por-
tion of the old debt that he himself had agreed to when she
had bought the land. Then, there was mercy. Adeline rebuilt
the tenant's home and sheds that had fallen into disrepair under the previous landlord, after which she was greeted not by
an ax but with expressions of thankfulness and joy.

This orchard became Adeline's refuge in Bosnia. It was
small and simple compared to her childhood home, Boyland

Hall, and her sister's retreat from London, Monk's Orchard, but it was hers. She was a Bosnian landowner; she was no longer a tourist or visitor, but a resident. With this purchase she found herself distanced one more step from the past she was leaving behind.

Adeline and her work, which had been so prominently featured in the British media during the years of the uprising, slowly faded from public view. In 1881, on December 26, she made a final personal appeal in *The Times* of London for funds for the orphanage; she had only received enough money the previous year to cover half of the £800 needed to run the school. Her name appeared twice more in papers in Britain in 1884, the first time as co-author of a letter published in *The Times* in support of a woman's right to suffrage (written with Sophia Jex Blake) and the second time in an unsigned letter in the *Pall Mall Gazette* entitled "An English Lady's Work."[78]

The latter described a visit by the writer to the *Zavod* and expresses her favorable opinion of the work there. English men and women, the article explains, have eagerly traveled all over the world spreading the values of their homeland, but "amid all this exuberance of zealotry... there are here and there curious instances of enthusiasm undiluted by any selfish trace of sectarianism, or even of patriotism." One of the examples of "these isolated cases of disinterested services for humanity apart from sect or nationality" was Miss Irby and her little school, which was in danger of being neglected. So non-partisan was the work that even young Orthodox priests came to Miss Irby seeking wives, saying, "All the girls at your school are such good Slavonic Orthodox; any you recommend will do for me." And, with an appeal for funds, the author asks, "Would it not be deplorable if a school like this were allowed to stop its work for want of funds?"

Despite this attempt to keep Adeline and her work in front of the British public, the collective memory was short. A.P. Irby and her little school were being forgotten.

One major change occurred within the *Zavod* in 1885: Priscilla returned to England permanently. It is easy to speculate as to why she left. Did she and Adeline have a disagreement that fragmented their working relationship? Was she overwhelmed with the stresses of Bosnian life? Did her political or religious opinions change in such a way that they were no longer compatible with Adeline and her mission? However, perhaps most likely, she felt she had completed the work she came to do.

The work had always been Adeline's first; she was the expert, the writer, the recognized name, the experienced traveler, the dreamer. For thirteen years Priscilla had labored to see that work accomplished on the plains of Slavonia, beneath the mountains of Dalmatia, and in the heart of Bosnia. Perhaps the work could have been done without her, but not to the same scale and quality. The money she raised, the letters she wrote, the friends and family she involved, the organization she added all contributed to the success of their relief work. How long would Adeline have lasted alone? No one can tell. Priscilla responded to the need, gave a decade of her life in service to the people of Bosnia, and then quietly returned home.

When she died in January 1912 not many of her relatives remembered her time in the Balkans. To the younger ones she was simply "Aunt Pris," who cared about humanitarian work and had a love for animals. Perhaps that was fitting. Priscilla had not come to Bosnia in search of recognition; she came because she believed it was right to help those in need. And that was exactly what she had done.

Within the walls of the *Zavod*, Adeline continued to pursue the mission that she and Georgina had first laid out in 1868 when they founded the Association for the Promotion of Education among the Slavonic Children of Bosnia and Hercegovina. They wrote in the first pamphlet advertising the association that "in the school which it is proposed to found, reading, writing, arithmetic, history, geography, plain work, cooking, and care of health, would be among the branches of instruction; but the principal aim would be to give the girls a sound, useful education, based upon the doctrine of Christ, and so not only to effect a gradual elevation of their intellectual and social condition, but also to prepare them to be the future teachers of their countrywomen." Already, several of the boys they had originally housed in Sarajevo were schoolmasters, and one recent female graduate had become the schoolmistress in her village. Sadly, each year, this noble mission became more difficult to accomplish.

The Austrian government, working to improve education throughout the country and bring it in line with the standards of the other provinces, introduced new requirements for schoolteachers. In order to be accepted to the *Preparandija*—the training school for teachers—a prospective candidate had to first pass an extensive test on a wide variety of topics that included algebra, geometry, logic, zoology, chemistry and botany. Adeline found it difficult to find enough suitable teachers to keep up with these demands. In a presentation to the 1893 International Congress of Education in Chicago she said, "It is evident that some of the subjects must be taught by the teachers or professors from the gymnasium or from the *Preperandija*, and I find the expense of these lessons is so great that it is doubtful whether I shall continue them."

Adeline, who would turn 62 the following December, was prepared to alter her dream of training schoolmistresses. She was not, however, willing to give up the *Zavod*. "The Home, the orphanage," she continued in her speech, "is as greatly needed as ever, and the true idea of a training school in its moral as well as intellectual bearing reaches beyond the mere equipment for school examinations." The school had never been simply about knowledge. It was about preparing young women to stand secure in the presence of the moral temptations of life and, through their good example, influence their neighbors to do the same.

In the shifting world of Austro-Hungarian controlled Bosnia and Herzegovina, the *Zavod* still had a purpose to fulfill. Adeline observed that along with the "civilizing" influence of Europe came a change in morals and culture. German dances and songs were replacing the *kolo* and traditional music. The Slavic culture that she had come to appreciate was slowly evaporating under the Germanizing influence of the occupying force. The *Zavod* could be a place where Slavic, Bosnian, Serbian culture could be celebrated and protected. As one historian noted, "Within Miss Irby's school her pupils took German lessons and were reminded all the time that this was a foreign language."[79] If Adeline could not send out schoolteachers, she would at least return the girls to their villages with a love for their country and their culture.

Adeline concluded her 1893 speech with these words:

> *When the examination is over, and the Home quitted, some friendly moral aid is sorely needed... for the girl teacher who is sent forth to sink or swim in the miry waters which over-flood every rank of society in Eastern Europe. The young schoolmasters and schoolmistresses have a wide influence for good or for evil, by their teaching and their example. They stand in the midst of temptations, for the most part wholly without uplifting aids around them, and without any adequate moral control.*

Adeline planned to continue, until the day of her death, to teach girls how to stand.

One friend remembered Adeline and her school, even to the very end. Florence Nightingale had always been a source of encouragement and exhortation for Adeline. When she launched her refugee work, Florence was there to help with the organization and fundraising. When she fell under the cloud of doubt, Florence was there to shine the light of truth into her life. When she needed a place of refuge in England, Florence was there at Lea Hurst. When she became tangled in the red tape of bureaucracy, Florence was there to call on her influential friends. Florence was a true and faithful friend.

Florence remembered Adeline even in death. When she died in 1910, she left £500—over half the yearly expense for the school—to Miss Irby and her work.

When Adeline spoke about the *Zavod* to an English-speaker, she called it "the Home." "Home" is a versatile word. In its simplest literal definition, a home is a place of residence. A home can be a building or an apartment, a town home or a mansion. It can also represent a geographical area or a city. A home is where one lives. But the word also has a figurative meaning: a mental or emotional state of refuge or comfort. Home is a place of belonging, a reality that defines and gives meaning. Perhaps that is why it was Adeline's preferred name for the school. It was a place where orphans could come to live, to belong, to be defined, to discover refuge and comfort. Even for those students who were not orphaned, the *Zavod* served as a second home, a place where they could better understand themselves.

This place that Adeline built as a school for young girls became, to her, a home. It defined her. It gave her meaning. For 35 years—three before the uprising and 32 afterwards—the *Zavod* was her home; a place in which she poured out all of her energy and, at the same time, was energized. She lived at Boyland Hall for only 20 years and then at Hyde Park Gardens for less than that. In no other city did she reside longer than in Sarajevo. Much like the students she served (How many over those 35 years?), when she saw the front door of the *Zavod*, she knew she was home.

In the time following the uprising, she spent £24,800* (assuming a steady cost of £800 per year) on the day-to-day expenses of the school, at least half of which she paid for herself. This did not keep her from also supporting the girls as they left the Home. Adeline gave dowries for their weddings, wrote letters of encouragement, offered wisdom when they needed it. If the *Zavod* was a Home, she was the kind-hearted mother sending her children out into the world. As Adeline grew older—the quick, bouncing steps of her youth replaced by a slow plod—she never ceased to spend time at home among her family. The children would climb up into her lap and press their cheeks against her palm. She would close her eyes and listen to their songs.

When at last the Home closed, the little baby girl, who had been only one year old when Adeline returned from Knin, was a 33-year-old woman. What would have happened to her had she not been brought to the Home? Perhaps she would have died. That would have been the most likely result. But, if she had lived, she would have always carried with her the questions: Who am I? To whom do I belong? Why am I here? These are the questions of an orphaned heart. But she was found. She did have a home. While there is no documentation as to what she became after leaving the *Zavod*, in what town she lived or whom she married, certainly, there was one thing she carried with her until the day she died: a sense of home.

---

* Over $2 million in modern equivalency

LOVE

I have found the paradox, that if you love until it hurts,
there can be no more hurt, only more love.
—Mother Theresa[80]

Ljubav ne pozna srednji put; upropasti ili spasi.
(Love knows no middle way; it destroys or saves.)
—Bosnian Proverb

WHEN I FIRST met Adeline, I thought of her story like a
dramatic international film. The plot had all the elements: war, politics, danger, intrigue. After two years, though,
I began to see another plotline emerge. Her life was a love
story.

The best love stories can often be the unexpected ones. In
truth, it is the surprise that draws us in. There is not much
compelling about a wealthy young man falling in love with
a wealthy young woman, or a dashing sports star marrying a
beautiful model. The heartwarming tales are about true love
triumphing over differences and against all odds. What kind

of story would *Romeo and Juliet* be had Romeo not been a Montague?

The entire romantic-comedy genre is based on the formula of unexpected love: the strong-willed female CEO falling for the delivery man, the boss's daughter running off with his competitor's son, the polar opposites discovering that opposites do, in fact, attract. These are the stories that endure: love across borders, love across nationalities, love across enemy lines, love across social divides, love above all, over all and conquering all. Most relationships come and go without much notice, but we build statues, erect monuments, and dedicate bridges in honor of unexpected love.

Could there be a more unexpected love story than the one between Adeline and the people of Bosnia? This is how I began to picture it:

> *Adeline, born into wealth and privilege, was groomed to spend her life as the lady of a lord, hosting lavish dinner parties, entertaining the wives of government officials and civic leaders, and enjoying the best that British society had to offer. She had a freedom that 99% of the world would never experience and could not understand. Yet, it was while enjoying that freedom traveling through Europe that she caught a glimpse of "him" for the first time. It was not love at first sight, but there was something about him that attracted her; he intrigued her in a way that the London elite did not. He was wild and confusing, but the very fact that she could not understand him made her curious and drew her in.*

As she began to learn more about him, her curiosity turned to sympathy. Despite a noble history, he so often found himself beneath the thumb of larger and stronger forces without anyone to defend him. In fact, her own people were a part of the problem. Perhaps she could use her power and position to help him out, give him a step up, and put him on a better path. All of this was out of a desire, of course, to help out a friend. She was just doing what anyone else in her situation would do.

But then, tragedy struck, and his very life was in danger. During this time, all other projects and passions faded out of view as she poured herself into nursing him back to health. Night after night she sat by his bed, day after day she fed him, her efforts the only thing standing between him and death. At some point during this period she began to realize emotions within herself that went beyond friendship. She began to love him.

When at last he was healthy enough to return home, she went with him. This was an amazing time for both of them; the trust she had earned during his sickness was a foundation to their relationship. The more time they spent together, the less she thought about home and the life she left behind. At last they were married.

Throughout their marriage, she worked tirelessly for his good, supporting and honoring him. Her greatest desire was to see him succeed. They grew old together and when, at last, she closed her eyes in death, they were buried side by side.

On Valentine's Day some friends went onto the university campus in Sarajevo with a huge red cut-out of a heart on which the words were written: "What does love mean to you?". For a couple of hours students wrote down, with pens and markers, what love meant to them. Of course, my friends heard every kind of answer: "love is pain", "love is beauty", "love is that thing we all want but can never find", "love is the meaning of life". One gentleman who, based on his advanced age and lack of Bosnian, was neither a student nor a Bosnian scribbled in his mother-tongue, "Love is sour cabbage." His was my favorite response, not because I think love is sour, but because love most often comes in the most surprising package. As one of my friends said, "Cabbage may be sour, but it sure does make some good *sarma*.*"

The best definition of love that I have found comes from Adeline's favorite book, the Bible. I appreciate it because it is simultaneously simple and impossible to fulfill, like love itself.

Love is patient and kind;
love does not envy or boast;
it is not arrogant or rude.
It does not insist on its own way;
it is not irritable or resentful;
it does not rejoice at wrongdoing,
but rejoices with the truth.
Love bears all things,
believes all things,
hopes all things,
endures all things.
Love never ends.

---

* Sarma is a traditional Bosnian dish made by wrapping cabbage or grape leaves around minced meat.

Unfortunately, for most of us, definitions do not change our lives. Knowing what to do, or in this case how to love, does not always result in love. I find that I learn much better from a good example than I do from a command or definition. But, there are not many examples of this kind of love in the world today. The world often seems to confirm what one other student wrote on the big red heart: "I just don't care."

Even examples have their limitations. Watching soccer does not make me able to play. Reading about Mother Theresa does not automatically make me compassionate. Seeing love in others does not make me loving. Perhaps what we need most of all, in order to really love, is to be loved. Perhaps Adeline's love for the South Slavs came from a love that she herself experienced. She loved, because she knew what it was to be loved. Her love story was a part of another, larger story.

In many ways, the Bible—the book Adeline read daily and distributed freely—is a love story. In the beginning of the story, God created people so that he could love them, that they could return his love, and together, they could share a loving relationship. However, the people he created weren't sure that they could trust their creator; they weren't certain that a relationship with him was the best life had to offer. Instead of returning the love that he gave, they chose to reject him and set out on their own. God knew that this would be disastrous for them, but wanting them to have the freedom to truly love, he let them have their way.

As the years passed by, the people God had created found new ways to be unloving towards God and towards each other. Since they had severed their connection with God, all their other relationships suffered: with themselves, with their neighbors, and with the rest of creation. Within the first few chapters of the story, love was nearly erased from the earth. Mankind was heading in a hopeless and helpless direction.

God had a rescue plan. He had a way to not only save his creation but to win their love. His plan was, like any good love story, an unexpected one. God knew that simply clarifying the definition of love would not help. He knew that giving them an example to follow would not help. The only solution was an extreme one. God would have to come down and rescue them himself.

Sacrificial love was the only answer to the problem. The one who created life itself was born as a helpless baby. The one who formed man out of the dust of the earth walked the dusty streets he had made. The one who lived in the perfect splendor of heaven had no home to call his own. The one without need was hungry, thirsty, and tired. What motivated this sacrifice? It was love. That was how John, a follower of Jesus, explained it. "This is how much God loved the world: He gave his Son, his one and only Son. And this is why: so that no one need be destroyed; by believing in him, anyone can have a whole and lasting life."[81]

This, according to the Bible, was God's rescue plan; he sent his Son to save his people. Saving them took more than the sacrifice of leaving heaven to come to earth. Jesus, who taught that we should love our neighbors as we love ourselves, also said that there is no greater kind of love than to give up your life to save a friend.

This love story required the tragedy of death. Not the kind of death found in Romeo and Juliet, in which two lovers give up their lives because they could not be together. Jesus gave up his life so that God and his people could be together. He died to destroy the barrier of rebellion that stood between God and his creation. At the end of the story, even death itself was defeated. The hero, Jesus, whose death was the ultimate sacrifice of love, came back to life again. Death lost out to love. God offered his people a new start so that they could experience his love, return his love, and live in relationship with him.

God's love restored and changed his people. John, writing towards the end of his life, had not moved past this idea of love. "This is how God showed his love for us: God sent his only Son into the world so we might live through him. This is the kind of love we are talking about—not that we once upon a time loved God, but that he loved us and sent his Son as a sacrifice to clear away our sins and the damage they've done to our relationship with God. My dear, dear friends, if God loved us like this, we certainly ought to love each other. First we were loved, now we love. He loved us first."[82]

Adeline knew this love story by heart. This love story shaped her heart. Is it surprising that her love story is full of sacrifice and selfless service when that was exactly the kind of love she, herself, had experienced?

For the past two years I have been driven by the question: Who was Adeline Paulina Irby? In the process of answering it, I discovered the more important question: *Why* did she do what she did? Why did she give up her upper class life in London? Why did she serve a people so foreign to her? Why

did she spend her own wealth to help others? Why did she remain firm in the face of adversity? Why? The only answer I
have found is love. A love she experienced became a love she
gave. She learned love from a loving God.

A LAMP WILL SHINE

15-17 Sept 1911

May some of this noble value come to us and inspire us in all of our work. Let her character remain among us, in our memories as a symbol of that which is the best in us and of all people.
—Ivo Andrić, about Miss Irby[83]

Through our fields, where the berries stand,
Tirelessly, as a sower God-given,
You shone underneath the continuous mist
All the stars of your heart and love.
—Aleksa Šantić, from *Miss Irby's Song*[84]

ADELINE DIED ON a Friday—early in the morning—succumbing to a sickness she had long endured in silence. Never one to draw attention to herself, she quietly spent the last years of her life within the walls of the *Zavod*, hiding her sickness from all but those closest to her.

She was prepared for this day. The year before she had

updated her last will and testament. Through it, she did in death what she had done in life: took care of the people around her. She set aside a yearly stipend of 1000 Kronen for four women and for the Vekić family; she allowed for the Rusić family to live in one of her houses rent-free for the rest of their lives and receive 300 Kronen yearly for other expenses. Through the Serbian Women's Society of Sarajevo she set aside a yearly amount of 500 Kronen and provided for the health and comfort of three widows and the children who had come through her school. Through the society *Prosvjeta* she provided an educational stipend for any of the girls who had come through her home. All remaining money, at the death of the trustees, would be split evenly between *Prosvjeta* and the Serbian Women's Society. She also made two personal requests—that all her personal letters and journals were to be "scrupulously and conscientiously burnt unread" and she was to be buried in the cheapest fashion, without songs, speeches, or ceremony in the Protestant cemetery in Sarajevo. One of those wishes was fulfilled, her papers were destroyed, but the death of "The Noble" was too great an occasion to quietly pass by.

The evening edition of the *Sarajevski List* carried an article the day of her death which began, "This morning, after a prolonged sickness and at a full age, one great noble woman's soul was released, the great cultural benefactress of our people, especially the Serbian-Orthodox, with whom she has, for the past forty years, invested her rare noble heart, her tireless labor and her immense material sacrifice in the support and education of orphaned Bosnian boys and girls in her institution in Sarajevo." Letters and flowers began arriving soon after from all corners of the country; newspapers and magazines were filled with stories about her life. Throughout the city of Sarajevo black cloth hung from windows and church bells rang to mourn her death. Despite her wishes, a service was held in her memory at the Orthodox Cathedral in Sarajevo and similar observances took place in five other Bosnian cities. Wreaths arrived from dignitaries and government officials throughout the region and condolences reached the English embassy.

This was a public time of mourning for many in Bosnia, but especially for the Serbian people of Sarajevo. The *Sarajevski List* article had accurately stated that Adeline's work had been "especially" with the Orthodox of Bosnia. Although she had opened the school to any young girls who would come, it was the orthodox community that first accepted her help and with whom she had gained trust during the uprising. During the final 20 years of her life, as the *Zavod* transitioned from a training school for schoolmistresses to a cultural school, her connection with the Orthodox of Sarajevo deepened. The community, who had initially rejected her, had come to think of her as their own. Under the rule of Austro-Hungary and in the years following the annexation of Bosnia in 1908, there were limited opportunities for the Serbian population to hold public expressions of their community. The death of "The Noble" was one opportunity that the authorities could not deny them. All Serbian institutions flew their flags at half-mast, *Bosanska Vila* declared on its front page "The good lady has died," and people came out into the streets to celebrate the life of their noble benefactress.

★   ★   ★

By one o'clock on Sunday, September 17, 1911, three hours
before the scheduled start of the funeral procession, a crowd
was already forming along Franje Josipa Street in front of
the *Zavod*. Grey clouds hung over the valley and the air carried the thick smell of rain. The mourners milled about on
the street and in the city park, their numbers growing as the
appointed hour approached, solemnly greeting one another
and quietly engaging in conversation. The men were dressed
in dark suits and hats, and many wore overcoats to guard
against the early fall chill. The women's dress varied, some
wearing black from head to foot. Others dressed in lighter
colors with flowers in their hats. The boys wore short pants
and coats, the girls their best dresses.

When the coffin emerged from the *Zavod* silence spread
over the assembly. The closed casket was laid in the school
courtyard and the officiating Protestant Pastor Ivan Schafer,
said a prayer. After a song from the choir *Sloga*, Adeline's
body was set in a funeral carriage, beautifully constructed
of dark wood and accented with gold, pulled by two black
horses. Atop the hearse were large garlands that spilled down
over the sides, the pink and red roses and the brightly hued
ribbons standing out above the unhappy procession. The funeral march was appropriately led by school children—not
from the *Zavod*, but from all over the city—snaking down
the road, from youngest to oldest: primary school boys, small
hands clasped together and flanked by their teachers; primary school girls, white school dresses cleaned for the occasion; senior girls, faces downcast by the understanding that
comes with age; older students from the trade school, secondary school, and high school; teachers in training from the
Preperandija. Coming behind the long column of children,

was one of the two carts loaded with wreaths, Pastor Schafer and his wife, and then the hearse itself. The current residents and students of the *Zavod* followed directly behind the funeral carriage. They wore white, in contrast with the crowd and perhaps at the direct request of Adeline. The small black bands around their arms and the kerchiefs with which they constantly blotted their tears visibly showed their grief. Following the women from the *Zavod* was the diplomatic core: English Consul Freeman and his wife, representatives of the Austro-Hungarian government, leaders within the Orthodox Church, members of the National Council, government advisors and department heads. After them, followed religious leaders and representatives of civic and social organizations. As the procession passed the *Zavod* and curved onto Čemaluša Street, the thousands who had been watching alongside the road joined the cavalcade. En masse, these people from all walks of society—old, young, rich, poor, male, female, Orthodox, Catholic, Muslim, Protestant—made their way west and then north to the Protestant Cemetery at Koševo to pay their last respects to their Noble.

As the throng crowded around the open grave and Adeline's body was lowered into the ground, it began to rain. Pastor Schafer ascended a small platform draped in black material that was set beside the tombstone and delivered the only speech of the afternoon:

In the name of the Lord, beloved,

Speaking at a funeral is an act of acknowledgement and comfort. On the funeral of the deceased, it would be enough to read her biography, especially from forty years ago, because that is the true acknowledgement for her. What will I add out of my weak words? Adeline had carved herself into human hearts year after year, day after day, of her lifetime, that the number of the grateful is thousands and the statements from all over the country clearly say that over her grave, crushed with grief stand together all of the Serbs of Bosnia and Herzegovina.

What great stance, what a wide horizon that defines her in her own goodness and all of her work. Not even the simplicity of confessionalism or the short breath of nationalism ruled her—she was a member of one Church, which thinks elevated, a child of a noble nation. She did not ask if the orphans spoke English or were they evangelicals by faith, but wherever she saw misery she helped.

Who doesn't know the story of the Good Samaritan? Here we have a Samaritan like the heart of our Lord Jesus Christ. And once she had felt the happiness of knowing what it means to be able to help the Lord, there was no other way for her. She understood the words of God, completely and utterly: What you've done to one of my little brothers, you've done to me as well.

The spark of eternal love, which God placed upon her soul, flamed at the aisle of love toward her neighbor, in fire that Charity and education would

*continue to keep and encourage. In spirit she
stands in the middle of this yard, in the middle of
all the Serbian people, and yells to you: 'Go and do
good!'—Amen.*[85]

Then, with a blessing, the grave was filled and Adeline's
body was buried beneath the Bosnian soil she had come to
call home.

As the crowd dispersed, two school-aged girls made their
way to the graveside, which was covered with a large gar-
land of roses. They stood alone in front of the tombstone and
cried. Carved into the large granite monument was a picture of Adeline in her old age and the words, in English and
Cyrillic, "Here lies the body of Adeline Paulina Irby, a great
benefactress of the Serbian people of Bosnia-Hercegovina."
Drying their tears, they stepped back, unsure what to do next.
At that moment, a photographer captured the scene, a juxta-
position of death and life. The dark grey headstone dominat-
ed the frame, the obvious intent of the photographer. One of
the girls stood at the foot of the cemetery plot with her arms
crossed over her abdomen, weight resting on her left foot, her
dark curly hair hidden beneath her white sun hat. The other,
dressed in a white knee-length dress, squinted in the direction of the photographer, fingering the kerchief in her hand.
Side-by-side they stood: the cold granite tombstone and the
schoolgirls. The latter was the only memorial Adeline desired.

As the sun set, the girls made their way home. That evening, before going to bed, they prepared for the next day.
They lined their shoes neatly at the door, stacked their books
on the table beside the bed, and draped their pressed school
dresses over the chair.

LIFE

The secret of man's being is not only to live
but to have something to live for.
—Fyodor Dostoyevsky, from *The Brothers Karamazov*

I have set before you life and death, blessing and curse.
Therefore choose life . . .
—*The Bible*, Deuteronomy 30:1[86]

ADELINE'S TOMBSTONE IS no longer in the Protestant cemetery where she was buried. When the graveyard was destroyed, the Orthodox Church requested to rebury her on their own ground. Her tombstone was moved across the street to Saint Mark cemetery. From time to time, I visit.

I pass through the cemetery gate as the sun emerges after a heavy rain. My shoes slosh in the wet grass as I make my way through the maze of worn, eroded memorials, at last reaching

Adeline's headstone. The black granite glistens in the afternoon sunlight. Standing in front of her grave, I think back through the previous two years: meeting Miss Irby, moving to a new country, writing a book. A mix of emotions swirls within me. I feel sadness, joy, gratitude, respect.

I think about my old home in the States. There are days I miss it, but I can see a home forming here. From the windows of our apartment I can see our new city, Sarajevo, spreading out in the valley below. I still miss my yellow chair. A less comfortable, flower-print armchair has replaced it. I still miss my friends. Their lives continue without us. They get married, have children, buy houses and celebrate birthdays without us.

I still miss my family. On the wall opposite the flower chair hang our family portraits. We had to wait a few months for them to arrive, then they stayed in boxes for a few more months, then we finally put them up where they belong. The day after we arranged them on the wall, I remember making myself a coffee, sitting in the flower chair as the early morning sun streamed in through the windows, and suddenly feeling more at home. I am starting to love my new city. I feel a sense of purpose here.

I think about the man I hitchhiked with after my bus broke down—the man with the washing machine drum on his backseat who seemed disinterested in the past. He was right. The thing about the past is that it has already passed. However, the past can shape the future. As the saying goes, "Those who cannot remember the past are condemned to repeat it." In Adeline's case, however, those who don't remember the past will, sadly, fail to repeat it. The world will benefit if Adeline's story is repeated. The past can shape the future for good. Learning about Adeline has already begun to shape my future. I am losing my ability to ignore the problems around me. I am noticing needs.

I think about the woman who sits on the steps at the bottom of our apartment. She asks where am I going every time I leave my house and where have I been every time I return. Every day, without fail, she asks for a cigarette even though each time I tell her I don't have any because I don't smoke. I am losing my ability to ignore her. Adeline's story is forcing me to notice. The other day I bought her a bag of groceries—some meat, cheese, bread, fruit. Now, when I leave my apartment she gives me a knowing glance—head tilted slightly down, eyebrows raised, wide grin—and raises her hand in an informal salute. She wants some potatoes and rice next time.

I think about Slavko and our conversation over coffee. His service to others flows directly out of his faith in God. God interrupted the plans he laid out for his life. The path he is on is leading him further and further from the selfishness of his past. I can see Adeline's story in his. Love leads people to greater sacrifice than fear ever could. Yet, the more a person is led by love, the less it feels like a sacrifice. Love led Adeline from her comfort in England to the deadly caves of Dinara. I want to understand this love better. I am excited about where it is leading me.

Looking at Adeline's gravestone, I think about death. She never wanted to be remembered in this way. She did not want to be remembered for her death, but for her life—a life that climbed mountains, confronted danger, sacrificed comfort for purpose, sought the good of others and laid itself down in service to her neighbor. For that reason, I don't visit the cemetery often. The best way I can remember her life is to live mine with honor, to open my eyes and take notice, to fulfill my purpose.

I never wonder anymore what I am supposed to do with my life. I know now. Live it. Live it in such a way that honors those who have come before. Live it in such a way that honors the God who created me. Live it in submission to the gravitational pull of God's plan and with love towards others. Live life the way Adeline did.

I think about the baby we lost last fall. The weight of death still remains, but life has the final word. Growing inside of my wife's belly is a new life. According to the doctor, the baby is a healthy girl. When I heard her heartbeat during the ultrasound I was filled with joy. Who will she become? Where will she go? What adventures will she face? What problems will she solve? Who will she help? Will she find her purpose? She should arrive only a month after the 100th anniversary of Adeline's death. A new Miss Irby.

The doctor asked us what we were planning to name the baby. We have already decided. We want to give her a name that she will have to live up to—a name that will inspire her. We are going to name her Adeline.

I think about the questions I had the day I met Miss Irby, particularly the one about our hereditary relation. I realize that I was asking a deeper question: To whom does Adeline belong? I wanted her to be my great-great-aunt so that, through heredity, she would belong to me. Maybe then, the purpose of her life would lend purpose to mine. Since then, I have discovered that we are only distant cousins. This was a disappointment at first. Now, it is not important. I am less concerned with how we are related in the past than how we will be similar in the future. We don't get to choose our families, but we can choose our actions. Perhaps Adeline belongs, not to those who share a bloodline, but to those who live out the values that compelled her life. What if compassion, perseverance, love, faith and sacrifice are the real indicators of ancestry? Then Adeline could belong to us all.

Turning my back on the tombstone I head towards the cemetery gate. Dark clouds still hang over the valley and the sun dances in and out behind them creating a patchwork of light across the graveyard—the beauty of life triumphing over death.

ACKNOWLEDGEMENTS

In order to accomplish a large task, like writing a book, you have to believe that it is possible. In my case, there were many people who believed in me more than I believed in myself. To those people I say, "Thank you, you were right."

Thank you:

> **Greg Ashworth**, for sending the email that introduced me to Miss Irby,

> **Bill Babione**, for planting the seed that became *Meeting Miss Irby*,

> **Brooke** and **Karen Butler**, for believing in this book and giving me the flexibility to write it,

> **Karen Bonnar**, for walking alongside me for an entire year, giving me honest input, and teaching me how to write,

> **Djordje Planinčić**, for being a good friend,

research helper, and resource translator,

Meca Kuc, for your excitement about this book from the first day I decided to write it,

Michael and **Brenda Brent**, for your unwavering support and a spot on your couch when I needed to get away to write,

Slavko Hadžić, for your friendship and trustworthy input,

Sandra Kasalović, for saving this book when I was close quitting,

Sean German, for helping me understand the publishing process,

Jonathan Trousdale, for your ideas both for the content and the design,

Steve and **Carrie Penley**, for your generosity,

Caleb Seeling, for helping me share Adeline's story with others,

Professor Edin Radušić, for the history lesson,

Professor Amila Kasumović, for working so hard to help your students understand the Reformation,

Prosvjeta in Sarajevo, for working to keep Miss Irby's memory alive,

Vanja Jovanović, for sharing a coffee and talking about Miss Irby,

The Historical Archive of Sarajevo, especially Saša, for bearing with my endless questions,

The National Archive of Bosnia and Hercegovina, for the wonderful pictures,

Dorothy Anderson, for diligently researching Adeline's life fifty years ago,

Andrew Parker, for a compelling design,

Mike and **Jasmin Morrell**, for fixing my grammatical errors,

Nicole Parker, for being my grammatical safety net,

My friends in Sarajevo, for welcoming my family into your city,

The students of Sarajevo, for being willing to talk about life with me,

SvakiStudent, for the privilege of working with a group that truly loves students,

262   MEETING MISS IRBY

Udruga Fokus in Croatia, Bosnia, and Serbia, for
your openness to this project,

Evanđeoska Crkva Bosne i Hercegovine, for your
positive presence in BiH,

Mladi Muslimani, especially **Aziz**, for taking
time to talk,

Tom and **Dea Irby**, my parents, for releasing me
to go, live life, discover, and explore,

Taylor Irby, for your unwavering support as I
spent time with "the other woman" this past year,
but most of all, for your love,

Sarajevo, for being a city full of history and
surprise,

Adeline Paulina Irby, for living a life worth writing about,

God, for writing such a beautiful story in the
world and allowing me to play a role in it.

NOTES

1. Robert Louis Stevenson, *The Amateur Emigrant* (Chicago, 1895) 67-68.

2. This quote is often misattributed to Mark Twain.

3. Emily Thornwell, *The Ladies Guide to Perfect Gentility* (New York: Derby & Jackson, 1856) 148.

4. Thornwell 148.

5. Peter Ackroyd, *London: The Biography* (London: Vintage, 2001) 591.

6. J.R.R. Tolkien, *The Lord of the Rings* (Houghton Mifflin, 2004) 74.

7. Theodore Roosevelt, *Through the Brazilian Wilderness* (Palladium Press, 1914).

8. G. Muir Mackenzie and A.P. Irby, *Across the Carpathians* (London: Macmillian and Co.,1862) 65.

9. *Carpathians* 150.

10. *Carpathians* 173.

11. Glenny, Misha. *The Balkans: nationalism, war, and the great*

powers, 1804-1999. P73

12. G. Muir Mackenzie and A.P. Irby, *Travels in the Slavonic Provinces of Turkey-in-Europe*, 1st ed. (London: Bell and Daldy, 1867) 55.

13. Andrić, Ivo, *Omerpaša Latas* (Sarajevo, 1977) 45.

14. *Travels*, 70.

15. *Travels*, 254.

16. *Travels*, 264.

17. *Travels*, 275.

18. *Travels*, 280.

19. *Travels*, 319.

20. Martin Luther King Jr., *Strength to Love* (Fortress Press, 1977) 48.

21. *Travels* 394.

22. *Travels* 404.

23. *Travels*, 394.

24. *Travels* 406.

25. *Travels* 259.

26. *Travels*, 479.

27. *Travels*, 492-493.

28. *Travels*, 484.

29. *Travels* 397.

30. C.S. Lewis, *The Four Loves* (Harcourt, Brace, 1960)

31. A letter from A.P. Irby published as 'Bosnian Fugitives,' *The Times*, 1 Feb 1876.

32. 32. Quoted by Dorothy Anderson, *Miss Irby and her Friends* (London: Hutchinson & Co., 1966) 64.

33. Quoted in Danica Kaća Čolović and Srđan Čolović, *The Noble Miss Irby* (Belgrade, 2004) 64.

34. Opening quote of Charles Buxton, *Memoirs of Sir Thomas Fowell Buxton* (London, 1849).

35. F.O. 95/1031

36. A.P. Irby, 'English Orphanage and training school in Bosnia, 1869-1893', Proceedings of the International Congress of Education, Chicago, 1893 (New York: National Educational Association, 1895) 900-903.

37. William Wilberforce, *A Practical View* (London, 1798) 454.

38. Charles Buxton, *Memoirs of Sir Thomas Fowell Buxton* (London, 1849) 109.

39. Petar Mirković, *Miss Adeline Paulina Irby* (Sarajevo, 1921) 32.

40. Travels 2nd ed., 44-45. Originally published in *The Times*

41. Reported by A.P. Irby (*Travels* 2nd ed., 43) from the account of Herr Fric, August 1876

42. A.P. Irby, 'Work among Bosnian fugitives', *Good Words for 1876* (London, 1876) 639.

43. 'Bosnian and Herzegovinian Refugees', *The Times*, 17 July 1877.

The article is a report from a meeting of influential leaders in London in support of the Bosnian and Herzegovinian refugees.

44. Arthur J. Evans, *Illyrian Letters* (London, 1878) 14.

45. A letter from Edward A. Freeman. Published in *The Times*, 6 Dec 1876.

46. W.J. Stillman in letter written 14 Nov 1876 and published in *The Times*, 16 Nov 1876.

47. A letter from Priscilla reprinted in Millicent Garrett Fawcett, Papers on the Eastern Question No. 11, 'The Martyrs of Turkish Misrule' (Eastern Question Association, 1877) 21.

48. Adeline's comments on their initial work in Slavonia (*The Times*, 1 Feb 1876) but also true of their start in Dalmatia.

49. *Illyrian Letters*, 6.

50. Mirkovic, 23.

51. Mirkovic, 29.

52. Henry Lyte, Abide with Me, 1847.

53. Mark 12:30-31. *Holy Bible: New International Version* (Zondervan, 1984).

54. Illyrian Letters, 224.

55. A letter from Dr. Ziemann. 'Bosnian Refugees,' *The Daily News*, 27 June 1877.

56. Dorothy Anderson. *Miss Irby and Her Friends* (London, 1966) 199-200.

57. *Illyrian Letters*, 227-8.

58. 58. *Illyrian Letters*, 60.

59. Dorothy Anderson. *Miss Irby and Her Friends* (London, 1966) 197.

60. 'London Correspondence,' *Freeman's Journal*, 24 Oct 1877.

61. 'Protest', *Poems of Problems* (Chicago, 1914) 154-155.

62. Romans 1:16-17. *The Holy Bible, English Standard Version* (Crossway Bibles, 2002).

63. A letter from A.P. Irby published as 'Bosnian Fugitives,' *The Times*, 1 Feb 1876.

64. A letter from A.P. Irby published as 'The Bosnian Fugitives,' *Manchester Guardian*, 19 Feb 1879.

65. A letter from Priscilla Johnston published as 'Suffering in Bosnia,' *Manchester Guardian*, 1 March 1879.

66. Advertisement for the Bosnian and Herzegovinian Fugitives and Orphan Relief Fund in *The Daily News*, 17 May 1879.

67. Petar Mirković, *Miss Adeline Paulina Irby* (Sarajevo, 1921) 32.

68. Dorothy Anderson. *Miss Irby and Her Friends* (London, 1966) 199-200.

69. Jesse Owens, *Blackthink: My Life as Black Man and White Man* (William Morrow, 1970) 150.

70. Margaret Evans, 'The English School in Serajevo,' *Monthly Packet of Evening Readings* (London, 1882) 207.

71. Mirkovic, 42.

72. Mirkovic, 43.

73. A.P. Irby, 'English Orphanage and training school in Bosnia, 1869-1893', Proceedings of the International Congress of Education, Chicago, 1893 (New York: National Educational Association, 1895) 900-903.

74. Quoted in Dorothy Anderson. *Miss Irby and Her Friends* (London, 1966) 198. Excerpt of a letter from Miss Nightingale to Mr. Gladstone, the beginning of July 1879.

75. Ivo Andrić, 'Miss Adelina Irby.' Reprinted in Danica Kaća Čolović and Srđan Čolović, *The Noble Miss Irby*, (Belgrade, 2004) 159-165.

76. Robert J. Donia, *Sarajevo: A Biography* (University of Michigan Press, 2006) 62.

77. A.P. Irby, 'Bosnia and its land tenure,' *The Contemporary Review* Volume LVI. July-December 1889 (London, 1889) 35.

78. 'An English lady's work,' *The Pall Mall Gazette*, 16 Aug 1884.

79. Dorothy Anderson. *Miss Irby and Her Friends* (London, 1966) 224.

80. Gwen Costello, *Spiritual Gems from Mother Theresa* (Twenty-third publications, 2008) 11.

81. John 3:16. *The Message: The Bible in Contemporary Language.* Eugene Peterson, ed. (NavPress, 2002).

82. 1 John 4:9,10,19. *The Message: The Bible in Contemporary Language.* Eugene Peterson, ed. (NavPress, 2002).

83. Ivo Andrić, 'Miss Adelina Irby.' Reprinted in Danica Kaća Čolović and Srđan Čolović, *The Noble Miss Irby*, (Belgrade, 2004) 159-165.

84. Excerpt from *Aleksa Šantić, Mis Irbijeva* (1911). Author's translation.

85. This is not the entire speech. Excerpts taken from Danica Kaća Čolović and Srđan Čolović *The Noble Miss Irby*, 132-133.

86. Deuteronomy 30:19. *The Holy Bible, English Standard Version* (Crossway Bibles, 2002).

Visit the website for more photos, maps, and other history
about the life and times of Miss Irby:

Photos

Maps

www.MissIrby.com

History

Blog

AUTHOR'S BIOGRAPHY

Joshua Irby is from Atlanta, Georgia, USA, but now lives in Sarajevo, Bosnia and Herzegovina. He graduated with an Industrial Engineering degree from the Georgia Institute of Technology but chose to work with students instead of becoming an engineer. He loves to travel, discuss philosophy, read books, and hang out with his friends. His greatest love, however, is his wife, Taylor, and their three children.

CPSIA information can be obtained at www.ICGtesting.com
Printed in the USA
LVOW130135070513

332559LV00002B/6/P